BRANDI D. JACKSON

Beyond Burnout: Embracing Authentic Success

Rediscovering Passion and Purpose in a World of Expectations

First published by Brandi's House 2024

Copyright © 2024 by Brandi D. Jackson

All rights reserved. No part of this publication may be reproduced, stored or transmitted in any form or by any means, electronic, mechanical, photocopying, recording, scanning, or otherwise without written permission from the publisher. It is illegal to copy this book, post it to a website, or distribute it by any other means without permission.

Brandi D. Jackson asserts the moral right to be identified as the author of this work.

First edition

Advisor: Marcus Black
Editing by Brandi Jackson

This book was professionally typeset on Reedsy.
Find out more at reedsy.com

Contents

Foreword		iv
1	Burnout: The Silent Alarm	1
2	Navigating The World Of Work	20
3	Validation: The Elusive Quest	33
4	The PTO Paradox	42
5	When Success Feels Wrong	52
6	Breaking Free: Overcoming The Stagnation Trap	62
7	Redefining Your Measure Of Success	73
8	The Courage To Quit	82
9	Positive Energy: Authenticity As Power	103
About the Author		111

Foreword

In a world that often demands more from us than we believe we can give, where the lines between personal fulfillment and professional obligations blur into indistinct gray, Brandi Jackson's "Beyond Burnout: Embracing Authentic Success" emerges as a beacon of hope and clarity. This remarkable work addresses a crucial issue of our time, one that resonates deeply with professionals across the globe who find themselves caught in a relentless cycle of overachievement and under-appreciation.

My good friend Brandi Jackson, the brilliant mind behind this transformative guide, is not just an author; she is a visionary. Her journey from the depths of burnout to the heights of authentic success is a testament to the power of resilience and the human spirit. As someone who has witnessed her incredible dedication and insight firsthand, I can confidently say that Brandi possesses an unparalleled ability to navigate the complexities of modern professional life. Her profound understanding of the delicate balance between passion, purpose, and expectations is what makes her the perfect guide for anyone seeking to reclaim their life from the throes of burnout. What sets Brandi apart is her authentic approach to professional development. She does not offer a one-size-fits-all solution but rather invites readers on a journey of self-discovery, encouraging them to redefine what success means on their own terms.

Her wisdom is both practical and profound, drawn from years of experience and a deep-seated empathy for those grappling with the pressures of today's fast-paced world.

"Beyond Burnout" is not just a book; it is a movement towards embracing a more meaningful, balanced, and fulfilling professional life. Brandi's words are a call to action, urging us to rediscover our inherent strengths and passions, to align our careers with our core values, and to ultimately live a life that is not only successful but also deeply satisfying. In these pages, you will find not only the tools to combat burnout but also the inspiration to pursue a life of authenticity and purpose. Brandi's guidance will empower you to break free from the constraints of external expectations and to embrace a path of genuine success. I am honored to introduce this extraordinary work by Brandi Jackson, a leader, a mentor, and a true expert in the art of navigating life's challenges with grace and resilience. As you embark on this transformative journey through "Beyond Burnout," may you find the courage to embrace your true potential and the joy that comes with living a life aligned with your passions and purpose. Because YOU CAN!

Marcus Black
  Bestselling Author
  Award Winning Speaker
  International Podcast Host

1

Burnout: The Silent Alarm

If you tell me you're burnt out, I'm not buying it—because to me, it's a loud, clear signal that you've been ignoring the real, uncomfortable truths about your own life. Burnout is more than just exhaustion; it's a wake-up call, a siren blaring through the fog of our daily routines, urging us to pay attention to the cracks we've allowed to form in our well-constructed facades.

Take it from me, a classic avoider who has spent countless hours burying my head in the sand, pretending that everything is fine while the world crumbles around me. I've mastered the art of distraction, drowning out the whispers of my inner voice with the noise of busy schedules and relentless obligations. But I've learned, often the hard way, that those whispers aren't meant to be ignored; they're the compass guiding us back to ourselves. So if you're feeling burnt out, it's time to pause, reflect, and confront those nagging truths you've been avoiding, because deep down, you know they hold the key to your liberation.

From a very young age, my life was intertwined with sports — the camaraderie, the competition, the early mornings, and the late nights. I was never the best on any of my teams. I can very much admit that now as a full-fledged half baked adult, but I was never the worst, either. In fact, I often found myself in that curious middle ground — a solid contributor, always present, always reliable, but never the star. Sometimes, I wondered what it would be like to be the best — the one everyone counted on, the one who always made the headlines, the one the crowd chanted their name. But I was also aware of the pressure that came with it. Even at a young age, I noticed that those who were considered the best carried the weight of the team on their shoulders. They were expected to lead, to excel, and to never falter. There was an unspoken assumption that they alone could tip the scales in favor of a win or a loss. And with that came a level of scrutiny that seemed exhausting, and as much as I thought about the glory of being the best, I also didn't want to face the burden of being the center of focus when things went bad.

If I'm being honest, a part of me now wonders if I didn't push myself to be the best because I never wanted to experience what the "best on the team" went through on and off the field — the pressure, the expectations, the assumption that their individual performance could determine the entire outcome of the game. It was a team sport, after all; one person doesn't change everything, technically. But the expectations of the best players felt disproportionate to what the rest of the team experienced, especially on days where the scoreboard showed a less than stellar performance. And by the time I reached high school, I was hearing from some of our greatest team members, the ones we all admired, "I feel burnt out."

Interestingly, the narrative wasn't just about physical exhaustion from endless practices or injuries that they seemed to carry like badges of honor. It was the mental strain that seemed to weigh the heaviest. Constantly, being in the spotlight meant they never really found solace or escape, even in moments meant for relaxation or celebration. The game was always on their minds; the pressure to maintain a certain standard didn't allow for a true break from this self-imposed vigilance. They even admitted to feeling jealousy toward teammates who, while contributing significantly to the team's dynamics, didn't carry the same individual pressure for victories or losses.

I'll never forget the time my softball team was down by one run, with two outs, a runner on third, and our best hitter at the plate. I was the runner on third, often chosen for these situations because I could make it those final 60 feet as quickly as possible, regardless of what happened — a wild pitch, a bunt down the first base line, anything. I had trained for moments like this my entire softball career. Our best hitter of the season was up, and although she'd been in a bit of a slump recently (it happens), she had always delivered when it mattered most, especially under pressure. Everyone on the team felt confident that she'd come through again and pull off the impossible. Do whatever it took to put the ball in play to give me a chance to score.

Simple enough. She'd done it hundreds of times before.

But I remember noticing something different in her eyes that day. It wasn't the look of fierce determination she usually had, the one that said, "I've got this." There was a hint of something else — doubt, maybe, or fatigue. It was hard to tell, but it didn't seem like she felt like the player she had always been. At 16 years old, I didn't fully understand what I was seeing. I had heard the coach tell her a few days earlier to take some time off, to rest and recharge, to find her love for the game again — as if her passion had somehow just been misplaced and could be easily retrieved, like an item in the lost and found. But when she came back, she didn't seem different. If anything, it felt like she didn't want to be there at all. It felt like she no longer wanted to be the star softball player everyone expected her to be.

You're probably thinking this had to end horribly — a strikeout, a missed opportunity, a lost game. But it didn't. Despite everything, she stepped up to the plate and hit a double. I sprinted home from third base, scoring the tying run. We walked it off in the next play and won the tournament. The crowd erupted, our team jumped up and down in celebration, and it felt like everything was back to normal. She had done what she always did: deliver in the clutch.

But what happened next shocked everyone. She turned down a scholarship offer to play at a Division I school — a dream opportunity for any athlete in our position. And then she quit the sport entirely, the sport she had been known for, the sport in which she was one of the best in the state. She just...quit. It was a decision that left everyone — coaches, teammates, her family — stunned. Why would she walk away from something she was so good at, something she had worked so hard for?

The decision took everyone by surprise, igniting endless conversations and debates among us. In hindsight, we had little to do with her choice, yet, in typical human fashion, we spent countless hours trying to decipher her motives without actually knowing her inner thoughts. How could someone so exceptionally gifted and naturally talented simply walk away from what seemed like a dream opportunity? On the surface, it appeared unfathomable. However, as the initial shock wore off and emotions settled, a different narrative slowly came to light— one that illuminated the nuanced complexities of personal happiness and fulfillment beyond the simplistic measures of external success.

Initially focused on the perceived loss of potential, we gradually considered the factors that might have influenced her decision. Her unexpected choice prompted deeper reflection on the pressures that come with exceptional talent—the relentless expectations to succeed, the constant scrutiny, and the sacrifices that often overshadow personal well-being. It became increasingly clear that her decision was not an impulsive abandonment of a promising future, but a courageous step towards finding genuine fulfillment.

For her, the decision wasn't about the accolades or expectations, but about reclaiming a sense of self that had been lost somewhere amid the practices, games, and constant pressure to excel. She started to share more openly about her feelings with those she trusted: how the joy she once felt on the field had slowly turned into a burden, how the sport had begun to constrain, rather than enhance, her sense of freedom and identity. These revelations shed light on the fact that, despite outward appearances, the life of an athlete can be as much about personal sacrifice as it is about glory and even with everything working in their favor.

I realized then that sometimes, even when you're winning on the outside, you can be losing something much deeper on the inside. It was the first time I truly understood that burnout wasn't just about being tired; it was about losing your passion, your drive, your reason for playing the game. And sometimes, even a win isn't enough to bring that back.

Reflecting on this moment of revelation, I began to see burnout not merely as a personal hurdle, but as a pervasive issue casting a long shadow over what should be something you're excited about. It was a profound understanding that struck me deeply, pushing me to reevaluate not only my approach to sports but also my life's priorities. Conversations about burnout, once dismissed as background noise, suddenly became critically relevant. The signs of burnout—stress, fatigue, and dwindling enthusiasm—were no longer abstract concepts but tangible realities that required attention. This recognition prompted a shift in my perspective, prompting me to seek balance in an environment that often glorified relentless perseverance and achievement. I realized that the narratives of those who walked away from their sport, like the teammate I deeply admired, were not just isolated stories of personal choice but vital lessons about the importance of self-care and the courage to redefine success. As I engaged more with these discussions, I discovered that burnout was not just an athlete's issue; it was a universal challenge affecting anyone who neglected their well-being in the pursuit of success.

Burnout.

It's a word that seemed to hover around the edges of conversations throughout my life, especially when I was growing up as an athlete. From a young age, I heard people talking about how kids could get burnt out even before they reached high school or college. It was as if burnout was this shadowy figure lurking in the background, waiting to pounce on anyone who pushed themselves too hard or went too far. It was always there, an almost mythical endpoint, a cautionary tale for those who dared to push the limits.

Over time, I began to associate burnout with a kind of point of no return — the idea that once you reached that state, you might never be able to pursue what you were passionate about again. It seemed like an irreversible condition, one that could rob you of your love for the game, the drive to compete, and the desire to excel. I remember hearing whispers about the top athletes, the stars of our teams, the ones everyone looked up to, being overworked, burning out, and eventually losing their desire to continue their athletic careers into college or beyond.

And you know what? It happened more often than I would have thought. A lot of those elite athletes I knew growing up, the ones who seemed destined for greatness, didn't go on to play in college. They quit. They stepped away from the sport at a time when the rest of us thought they'd be stepping up to the next level. It was confusing, even shocking. How could they walk away when they were so close to achieving what so many of us dreamed of?

Looking back, I realize now that burnout wasn't just some vague concept or distant threat; it was a genuine experience that impacted many of the most talented and driven people I knew. The ones who we thought had everything — talent, skill, and opportunity — were the very ones who seemed to fall victim to it. They had been the stars, the best on the field, the ones who carried the team. Yet, one by one, they quietly left the game behind, often with no grand explanation or farewell.

I used to think burnout meant just being tired or physically exhausted, but I've come to understand it's so much more than that. It's about emotional exhaustion, a kind of deep, pervasive fatigue that affects your very will to continue. It's the loss of passion, the erosion of joy, and the heavy weight of expectation. It's the fear that maybe, just maybe, the thing you loved most is no longer the thing you want to do. And for those who were once seen as the best, that realization can be the hardest thing to face — and even harder to admit.

It puzzled me, honestly. Why would someone who had worked so hard, someone with so much talent, just walk away from it all? Sometimes I wondered if there would have been something

I could have done to help them through those moments, something I could have said or done to ease the weight they were carrying. I saw how much they had sacrificed, how much they had invested in being the best, and it seemed tragic to me it all ended in a way that felt so unfulfilling for them.

I saw firsthand how much they had sacrificed over the years, how much time and energy they had invested in becoming the best. Early mornings, late nights, grueling practices, and endless games — they gave up so much for their sport, often at the expense of other parts of their lives. They missed out on social events, family time, and even just the freedom to relax and be a kid. All of it was done in the pursuit of greatness, to reach the next level, to fulfill a dream. Yet, for so many of them, that journey ended not with the triumph they deserved but with a quiet decision to leave it all behind.

They had reached a point where the love for the game was overshadowed by the exhaustion of the relentless grind. It was heartbreaking to see these athletes, once filled with so much joy and excitement for their sport, lose the very thing that made them shine. To me, they were still champions, still the people who had inspired me and so many others, but I couldn't help feeling that they had been cheated out of the ending they deserved, but the real question was, was it an ending they actually wanted or one everyone else wanted for them.

Sometimes, I wondered if burnout was a failure by everyone around them — teammates, coaches, friends — who couldn't see the warning signs or didn't know how to support them better. Could we have done more to help them balance the pressure, to remind them of the joy in what they were doing, to make it okay for them to step back, breathe, and find their love for the game again? I don't know. But I do know that I wish things had been different for them. I wish I had understood then what I know now about burnout — that it's not about weakness or giving up, but often about being so overwhelmed that you lose sight of why you started.

I'll never stop wondering if there was a way to rewrite those endings — a way to help them find a path back to what they loved, to the things that made them feel alive. And maybe, just maybe, it's a lesson that the rest of us can still learn: how to recognize when someone is struggling, how to offer a hand when the weight becomes too heavy, and how to help each other find our way back to the things that bring us joy even if it means leaving the thing that we all thought they loved.

When I entered the professional world and started hearing the same concept — burnout — used in relation to work, my initial thought was: "Okay, this just means you quit your job, right? It means you stop trying." In my mind, burnout was synonymous with leaving, with throwing in the towel, metaphorically. But as I encountered it more, especially in one-on-one conversations with colleagues who seemed unhappy, I realized it was more complex, even more complex than what I had learned burnout to be as a young athlete. My peers and team members would tell me they felt burnt out and just needed some time off; every conversation about burn out was met with the same recommendation – take some time. And I began to wonder: if burnout is defined as a form of exhaustion from feeling constantly overwhelmed, why would a trip to a beach be the end all be all solution?

The reality is, a break doesn't change the situation you're coming back to; it doesn't change what's causing your burnout from going away. To be honest, I started to think that when people said they were burnt out, especially in a professional setting, it was a cop-out. A universal answer that was more acceptable than saying what they were really thinking.

I've worked in startups my entire career, almost by accident, but it's an accident that has shaped everything about how I work and see the world. Startups are a unique environment; once you find yourself in that world, there's a certain addictive thrill that comes with it. There's something about the uncertainty, the unknown, that becomes oddly compelling. You find yourself constantly asking, "Will we make it through the month? How long will this job even last? Are we already out of money, or can we push through just a bit longer?" For most people, that level of instability would be exhausting, even terrifying — a nightmare they'd do anything to avoid. But for me, it's become a part of who I am.

In a way, I love that kind of uncertainty. I thrive on it. There's a strange sort of energy that comes from never really knowing what's going to happen next. It makes every day feel like a new challenge, a new puzzle to solve, and there's an excitement in that. Sure, there are moments of panic and stress, times when you're not sure if you'll have a job next week or if the company will still be around in a month. But there's also a kind of freedom in it. There are no routines that feel set in stone, no monotony that feels like it's crushing your spirit. Every day is different. Every problem is new. Every success feels like a victory against the odds.

I've realized that I don't do well with the constant, with the predictable. There's a part of me that craves the unknown, that loves waking up, not entirely sure what the day will bring. It keeps me on my toes; it forces me to think creatively and adapt quickly. At the same time, though, I'll admit that it can be exhausting in its own way. There are days when I long for a bit of normalcy, when I wish I could predict the week ahead with some certainty. I love it and I hate it, sometimes in the same breath.

The truth is, working in startups is like living in a constant state of flux, where the ground never feels entirely stable beneath your feet. But there's something about that instability that brings out a different side of you. It pushes you to your limits, makes you test yourself in ways you never thought possible. It's not just about having a job or building a company; it's about the challenge, the growth, the constant learning. And I think that's why I've stayed. Because there's something undeniably captivating about always being on the edge of something new, something unknown, and knowing that you have to be ready to leap at any moment.

So yes, I've worked in startups my entire career, almost by accident. But in that accident, I found a place where I feel truly alive, where I feel challenged every day, where I've learned to embrace both the chaos and the calm, the love and the hate, all at once.

My first startup experience in NYC began with a company that initially focused on marketing services. It was an exciting venture, full of innovation and the promise of growth run by a group of people with the average age of 30. However, as the market evolved and our understanding of client needs deepened, we shifted gears and transformed into a consulting firm. To put it simply, we were adapting to survive, trying to find our niche in a competitive landscape.

About four months after I moved to New York City and started this job, the CEO called an all-hands meeting. The atmosphere was thick with tension and unspoken concern, I didn't realize it then but the signs that we were in trouble were written all over the office, starting with the change of coffee from being a specialty blend from a small mom and pop shop in Brooklyn to Folgers. Nothing against Folgers but...a change in office amenities is your first red flag that things are going south. The CEO sat us all down and delivered the news: we were 60 days away from closing our doors for good. The financials were grim, and the runway was short. He told us we'd all need to be ready to fight if the company was going to make it. He emphasized that this battle wouldn't be easy and that he understood if anyone didn't want to go on this journey—there would be no hard feelings if someone decided to find another job.

I never once thought about leaving. The idea of abandoning ship when the stakes were highest didn't sit right with me. I was invested—not just financially, but emotionally and professionally. The next 30 days were truly a whirlwind. We worked tirelessly, often late into the night and early mornings, fueled by caffeine and sheer determination. The hours we put into turning that business around were absolutely insane. We brainstormed new strategies, reached out to every potential client we could think of, and overhauled our entire business model in record time.

But what struck me most was that not once did I hear anyone who stayed mention feeling burnt out. You'd think working around the clock with an actual ticking time bomb—60 days until closure—would cause burnout, but it didn't. How is that possible? You'd assume that this was a recipe for disaster. For a company wide burnout. But it didn't. Why?

I believe it was the collective sense of purpose and camaraderie that kept burnout at bay. We were all in the trenches together, united by a common goal that went beyond personal gain. The adrenaline of the challenge, the possibility of saving something we all believed in, energized us. Each minor victory fueled the next effort. There was an unspoken understanding that what we were doing mattered, not just to the company, but to each of us personally. The alignment of our individual passions with our professional roles created an environment where, despite the exhaustive workload, burnout didn't take hold.

In retrospect, it taught me a valuable lesson about the difference between working hard out of obligation and working hard out of passion. When you're deeply invested and believe in the purpose of your work, the usual factors that contribute to burnout—stress, long hours, high pressure—affect you differently. They become challenges to overcome rather than burdens to bear. That experience has shaped how I approach work ever since, reminding me that purpose and passion can sustain you even in the most trying times.

The environment was stressful, but there was also an incredible sense of purpose, a feeling that every action counted, that we were all in it together, fighting for something that mattered. In that context, it seemed like no one even had the time or the mental space to feel burnt out. We were too busy, too focused on the goal, too driven by the desire to make it to the next day. And yet, just a few months later, when the company stabilized, and the frantic energy subsided, I started hearing the word again: burnout. When the tide turned, when things got better, people started to sit in the new reality of their roles and despite having less, the talk of burnout grew more. While the energy had been high trying to turn around a sinking ship, once the ship was righted and new roles and responsibilities set in for the new chapter of the business, people stopped feeling the alignment to the shared mission; they stopped connecting to the new vision of the company. And suddenly they spent days trying to fit a square into a circle.

As my career path continued, this conversation around burn out became as standard as the constant need to fundraise for survival.

Startups, by nature, are unpredictable — they go through constant changes, ebbs and flows, and job roles shift overnight without notice. If you haven't worked at a startup before, it can be a lot to handle. What you sign up for isn't usually where you end up a handful of months later. When I joined a company in my late 20s who was building what they called a utopian for a product and a company, I should have expected the worst. There is no such thing as a one utopian for everyone. There especially is no such thing as a utopian for a company who is for profit and depends on venture capital funding for its survival. One day, a manager came to me and said she was feeling burnt out. The company was going through a huge growth spurt, a financial influx, and job expectations were rapidly transforming to meet the expectations that looked great on paper for fundraising but was almost physically impossible to accomplish. I looked at her and asked, "Are you truly burnt out? When you say you're burnt out, what are you really saying to me?"

She replied she felt like she couldn't get anything done — that there wasn't enough time to do the things she wanted to do. That was the key phrase: the things she WANTED to do. She was behind on tasks that had been added to her job description that she hadn't signed up for. She felt there wasn't enough time, but there was. It just wasn't what she wanted to be doing.

This is where many CEOs get frustrated — when people say they're overwhelmed or can't get things done, it's usually because they don't want to do certain things. If you're doing what you love, you get it done, no matter how much there is. In her case, everything she was originally hired to do was being done; it was the additional tasks she hadn't signed up for that weren't getting done. The things she had never agreed to do but had been told, for the betterment of the company, she needed to do.

This conversation turned from a performance review into something like a therapy session. She asked for time off because she felt burnt out. But when we dug deeper, it wasn't really about being overworked. The tasks she didn't want to do — managing the front desk, running payroll, handling food service, cleaning bathrooms — these were the things that were burning her out, not the core aspects of her original job, like planning events and socializing with members. I told her, "If I give you two weeks off, you know that all these tasks you don't want to do will still be here when you get back, right?"

That was a moment of realization for her. She admitted, "You're right. Taking a vacation doesn't change the fact I don't want to be a floor manager here. I signed up to do something else entirely."

And she was right. The reality was, the job had changed, and a vacation would not alter those new expectations. The company and business had shifted in a way where what was needed wasn't what she ever signed up to do. And in typical startup fashion, we'd shifted her reality without asking her. But if she didn't want to do the new job as it was designed, the other reality was there wasn't a place for her anymore, at no fault of her own.

So, I told her, "Take the time off, but ask yourself if you still want to be here, because this is the job now, and it won't change." It made me think — is burnout really about being overworked, or is it about not wanting to do what you're doing anymore? Is it really burnout, or is it a reluctance to admit that you don't want to be in this job or situation? Is it about knowing you need to change your reality but being afraid to do or say so?

The conflict, especially for those who have been at a startup since its early days, is deeply rooted in a complex mix of emotions and obligations. When you've been part of a company from its inception, you feel a profound sense of loyalty—not just to your role, but to the entire team and the mission you've all been striving to accomplish. You've witnessed the company's journey from a mere idea to a functioning entity, and that shared history creates a strong bond. However, as the company grows and evolves, so do its needs and structures. Roles that were likely never clearly defined to begin with start to blur even more, and responsibilities shift in ways you might not have expected because the business needs, goals, and priorities shift.

But things change. Startups are inherently fluid environments, and the agility that makes them exciting can also lead to unforeseen challenges. People burn out, and it's not necessarily because they have too much work on their plates. Often, it's because they feel misaligned with the direction the company is taking or the new responsibilities they're being asked to shoulder. They are expected to do things they didn't sign up for, tasks that might not play to their strengths or passions. This misalignment creates internal conflict and stress.

And that's the trap many find themselves in. We get so caught up in staying loyal, in proving we can handle any challenge thrown our way, that we ignore the signs that we're not doing what we want or need to be doing. There's a fear of letting the team down or being perceived as not committed enough. So, we push aside our own needs and continue to take on roles that drain us, all in the name of dedication.

In this relentless pursuit to support the team and fulfill

evolving expectations, we often neglect our own well-being and professional satisfaction. We might tell ourselves that it's just a phase, that the discomfort is temporary, and that our loyalty will eventually pay off when the company succeeds. However, ignoring these feelings can lead to a deeper sense of dissatisfaction and, ultimately, burnout.

It's important to recognize that being loyal doesn't mean you have to sacrifice your own happiness or career aspirations. Open communication is key. By expressing your concerns and discussing your role with leadership, you may find opportunities to realign your responsibilities with your skills and interests. After all, a startup thrives on the passion and energy of its team members. When everyone is engaged and working in roles that suit them, the entire company benefits.

So, while loyalty and dedication are admirable qualities, they shouldn't come at the expense of your own fulfillment. It's crucial to be honest with yourself about what you want and need from your work. Paying attention to these signs can help prevent burnout and ensure that you're contributing to the team in the most meaningful way possible.

Another example comes to mind with a peer I worked with, let's call him Sam. He was one of the best financial analysts I'd ever worked with. The kind of guy who could look at a spreadsheet for five minutes and tell you exactly what was wrong, where the errors were, and how to fix them. A real numbers whiz. But about a year into working with him, he seemed...off. Less engaged, less interested, just going through the motions. One day, he told me he was burnt out. I asked him to define what he meant by burnout.

He said, "I feel like I'm on autopilot. I'm not learning anything new. I'm not being challenged. I come in, do my job, and leave, and I feel like I'm wasting my time."

That struck a chord with me. He wasn't saying he had too much work; he was saying he had too little of the right kind of work. He wanted to be challenged, to grow, to feel excited about what he was doing. But instead, he felt like he was stagnant, like his skills were being wasted on tasks that didn't push him forward.

I realized then that burnout often stems from a sense of misalignment — when your skills, passions, and the work you're doing aren't in sync. When what you're doing feels like a waste of your time or a misuse of your talents, that's when burnout creeps in. It's not always about the amount of work; it's about the kind of work.

Looking back, I see burnout is more complex than just being tired or overwhelmed. It's about feeling disconnected from the work you're doing, feeling like your efforts are going towards something that doesn't matter to you, or feeling like your skills are being wasted. It's about a lack of purpose, a lack of passion, a lack of alignment between what you're doing and what you feel you should be doing.

Burnout isn't a failure; it's a signal. It's a sign that something needs to change — either in the work itself or in the way you're approaching it. It's an opportunity to reassess, to realign, to figure out what really matters to you and how to make that a part of your daily life.

I've come to understand that burnout is often about misalignment — between your passions and your work, your values, and your daily activities. It's a call to look deeper, to understand what truly drives you, and to find ways to make that a part of your reality. So, the next time someone tells me they're burnt out, I'll ask them, "What do you really mean by that?" Because more often than not, there's something deeper going on, something that needs to be addressed — not just with a break, but with a realignment of what they're doing and why they're doing it.

And maybe, just maybe, that's the key to avoiding burnout altogether: finding that alignment, that balance, that sense of purpose that makes all the hard work feel worth it.

2

Navigating The World Of Work

When you ask people about the idea of working, there is a commonly held belief that working experiences can be broadly categorized into two distinct types: working for oneself and working a traditional corporate nine-to-five job, or working for someone else. This dichotomy, while seemingly straightforward, often oversimplifies the complexities of different work arrangements.

Which I learned quickly in my own work experience.

For many, the notion of a nine-to-five job conjures images of rigid schedules, clocking in and out, and clearly defined boundaries between work and personal life which may have been more obtainable and true before we were able to carry work on our phones. However, my own career trajectory does not neatly fit into this conventional framework, and I doubt it ever really will since I tend to work in industries and for companies that don't fit a traditional mold. In fact, most of them are trying with all their might to break tradition in whatever industry they're trying to disrupt. Disruption and innovation are at the heart of any startup, after all.

My professional journey has been characterized by a mix of self-employment and roles within various startups, and I've come to realize that the traditional nine-to-five job, as commonly imagined, has not been a part of my career experience. Reflecting on my early career, I recall my stint right out of college at a law firm, where I encountered a work structure that was, in some ways, more rigid than the flexible environments I would later work in, but while it presents as a typical 9 to 5, anyone that has worked in a law firm as a supporting team member will say with their whole chest it's anything but. As a paralegal, my hours were dictated by the demands of the partner I supported, who often worked beyond the standard 40-hour work week; they worked beyond a standard 80 hour work week in most cases. In turn, my own hours extended well beyond what could be described as a conventional nine-to-five; more like 7am to 9pm, weekends and holidays included.

The law firm environment, while structured, did not offer a clear-cut distinction between work and personal time. My weekends were frequently occupied by checking emails and addressing urgent matters because if my group of law partners was working, I was expected to be working as well. The law rests for nothing, especially in the oil and gas industry. This blurred boundary between work and personal life became a theme throughout my career, particularly as I transitioned into roles at startups, where the concept of a traditional nine-to-five job is virtually non-existent. Most companies don't know what 9am is and most definitely don't end at 5pm.

Startups, especially those in their early stages—pre-seed, Series A, Series B, Series C—often embody a work culture that differs vastly from traditional corporate environments. Most startups begin with a core team all willing to do whatever it takes to make their dream a reality and that energy filters down to every hire especially if the company is constantly trying to survive. The excitement of contributing to groundbreaking projects and having a seat at the table is often accompanied by the understanding that work will inevitably bleed into personal life. I've actually been asked in interviews if I have things in my personal life that may impact my ability to be available at any moment especially when I was supporting an executive or Founder. I actually had a friend who had a contract that said they had to be available 24/7 and that wasn't at all an exaggeration. Now, don't get me wrong, in some instances that availability makes sense. Say a PA to a celebrity. But, in hindsight, having that kind of power over someone in a business setting can be more likened to a power trip more than a necessity. But I digress.

The startup culture walks a thin line between fostering innovation and becoming toxic through the expectations it places on its teams. On one hand, startups thrive on their ability to innovate quickly and adapt to changing market conditions. The flexibility and creativity that come with startup environments can lead to groundbreaking advancements and significant industry disruptions. In turn, it can truly accelerate your career, quickly moving you into a leadership role. I was a Head of something before I could legally rent a car which was exciting to say, but a truly overwhelming experience to go through. There is no way to truly prepare you to manage your peers when you're still learning how to manage yourself. This culture of constant innovation can also sometimes create a toxic work environment where the pressure to perform and the demand for excessive work hours become the norm. The constant hustle and grind mentality can lead to an unsustainable work-life balance, where employees are expected to be available around the clock and because that's the accepted culture, it becomes a "problem" if you want to operate in a different capacity. You become the problem and no one wants that so you conform to the grind and hustle culture that isn't sustainable for anyone.

This tension between fostering innovation and avoiding toxicity is a critical aspect of startup culture. While the drive for rapid growth and breakthrough ideas can be incredibly motivating, it can also lead to unrealistic expectations and a lack of boundaries between work and personal life. The pressure to deliver results constantly can lead to the conversation around team members being burnout and employees being dissatisfied. Nine times out of ten, it leads to conversations of letting those people go because they can't "handle it" or those people being told that they aren't a fit and they should look for other places to work. As if they are the problem and not the actual culture itself. The very qualities that make startups exciting—flexibility, dynamism, and a focus on innovation—can also contribute to a high-stress environment that may undermine employee well-being.

This reality can be particularly jarring for individuals who come from more traditional corporate backgrounds, where work hours are more defined and boundaries between work and personal life are more distinct. The reality of being constantly on call and managing responsibilities that extend beyond conventional job roles can quickly overshadow the initial appeal of working in a startup, with its promise of flexibility, flat organizational structure, and the promise of being a part of something bigger than yourself.

Remember the utopian company I mentioned in the previous chapter? Initially, the thrill of contributing to something innovative eventually gradually gave way to a deep-seated sense of burnout. Or, what I thought was burnout, but learned through that process, it was much more. It wasn't my first startup, not by a long shot, and like every startup I'd joined in the past, it had its promises of excitement and rapid growth, and initially captivated me. I was invigorated by the idea of being at the forefront of something new and impactful, eager to dive in and contribute my all. The energy was infectious, and the prospect of shaping something from the ground up was exhilarating.

However, as time passed, this initial excitement began to wane. What had once been a vibrant drive to excel and make a significant impact slowly morphed into something far less inspiring—resentment. The constant pressure to perform, with no clear delineation between work and personal life, began to take its toll. The startup's relentless pace meant that there was always more to be done, more to achieve, and the boundaries that typically safeguard personal time became increasingly blurred. My weekends, which once served as a much-needed sanctuary for personal rejuvenation, began to feel like just another extension of work. My days started at 7am and ended well after 11pm most nights. If it wasn't something with my team it was demands from the executive team wanting us to move faster yet wanting everything we did to be perfect. An impossible ask - there is no such thing as perfect even if that was the public's perception of the company and the brand.

This encroachment eroded the very space that was supposed to provide a respite from the demands of the job. What used to be a time for unwinding and disconnecting from work turned into a period where I found myself constantly tethered to my phone, addressing issues, or preparing for the next workday. Even when I was asleep, I was dreaming about work. There was always a fire somewhere waiting for me to put it out. It's worth noting that these moments of work intrusion into personal time hadn't bothered me in the past. Earlier in my career, I had been more flexible, accommodating work demands even on weekends, seeing it as part of the necessary grind and excitement of being involved in a startup. But as the demands increased and my personal boundaries continued to be tested, the novelty of this constant connectivity wore off. The once-tolerable intrusion became a source of deep frustration, transforming what had been a manageable aspect of the job into a significant source of stress and dissatisfaction.

As the pressure mounted, the excitement I had once felt about the startup's potential began to transform into a lingering bitterness. The sense of enthusiasm that had driven me to give my best now felt overshadowed by frustration. The tasks and responsibilities that had initially sparked joy and a sense of purpose now seemed like burdens. Each project that once excited me now felt like an additional weight on my already strained shoulders. I found myself increasingly avoiding Slack messages, dreading the constant ping of notifications that seemed to signify more work piling up. Meetings with the team I managed, which used to be a highlight of my day, became something I dreaded, as I no longer looked forward to the interactions that once invigorated me. The sound of my phone ringing filled me with a sense of dread, as it often signaled yet another issue to address or an urgent request. The growing aversion to these once-familiar aspects of my role was a stark indicator of how the initial excitement had been eroded by mounting stress and a deepening misalignment with my personal values.

But it wasn't because I couldn't handle it. I'd handled it for years before this and would, spoiler alert, handle it in the future. It was something about this place, this moment, where the feelings of not being able to handle it started to surface even if I couldn't figure out why. The expectations of this particular company were nothing I wasn't used to; in fact, they were quite similar to the demanding environments I had navigated throughout my career. The high-pressure, fast-paced nature of the work was familiar territory for me. I had thrived under such conditions before, often finding a sense of fulfillment in overcoming challenging obstacles and delivering results. So, part of me struggled to understand why, despite my experience and the skills I had developed over the years, I couldn't seem to summon the same drive and enthusiasm that had fueled my performance in the past.

I grappled with this internal conflict, questioning why I wasn't able to maintain the level of engagement and excitement that had previously been a hallmark of my professional life. The work was undeniably stressful, but it was also inherently complex and intriguing. Solving these intricate problems had once been a source of exhilaration, a part of what had drawn me to startups in the first place. Yet, as time went on, the excitement of tackling these challenges faded, and what had initially been stimulating work began to feel like an overwhelming burden. It was so bad, I couldn't even get myself to want to go to work but I couldn't not go to work so I felt truly trapped.

It didn't start this way, but it was how it ended. The transformation from enthusiasm to disillusionment was both disheartening and perplexing. I had hoped that the intense pressures and high expectations would be met with the same level of passion and dedication that had fueled my past successes. Instead, I found myself struggling to stay engaged, my once-enjoyable tasks now feeling like they were sapping my energy rather than fueling it. The mismatch between my early excitement and my eventual dissatisfaction left me searching for answers, trying to reconcile how I had gone from thriving in similar environments to feeling overwhelmed and unfulfilled in what was, on paper, a familiar and expected setting.

At first, I attributed these feelings to burnout—a temporary phase that could be alleviated with some time off or a change in routine. However, it became increasingly clear that this wasn't just about being overworked or needing a break. Nothing I did worked, no time away was erasing the reality that existed with the place I spent over 10 hours a day helping build. What I was experiencing was a deeper, more fundamental misalignment between what the company stood for and what I wanted to be a part of.

How did I figure it out? We had a team building exercise where we had to write our own eulogy, as morbid as that sounds. That exercise brought to light that it wasn't the work itself, it was everything the work stood for and what the work was helping contribute towards. I was building a company and contributing to the success of leaders and founders and I didn't align with at my core. This was the first time in my career I'd truly experienced this; the first time I realized I was trying to fit a circle into a square and it would never work.

As I spent more time reflecting on my role and the company's evolving direction, I realized that the root of my discontent lay in this misalignment. The startup's culture, which had initially seemed vibrant and dynamic, began to reveal itself as increasingly misaligned with my own values and aspirations.

For the first time, my personal values and the value I placed on work were shifting, and this change was having a profound impact on how I showed up day to day. Previously, my identity and sense of purpose were deeply intertwined with my professional role. I had prided myself on my ability to excel under pressure, to push through challenging times, and to find satisfaction in overcoming obstacles. My work was a significant part of who I was.

However, as my personal values began to evolve, so did my perspective on work. I started to prioritize aspects of my personal life that had previously been secondary to my career ambitions; secondary to the ambitions of the leaders I worked alongside. The boundaries between work and personal time, once fluid and flexible, began to take on greater significance. I started to recognize the importance of truly aligning with the values of the company beyond the title I carried or the salary I was making.

This shift in values directly impacted how I approached my job. Where I had once been enthusiastic and dedicated, I now found myself struggling with feelings of resentment and frustration. The relentless pressure and constant demands that had once fueled my drive now felt like an encroachment on my newly cherished values. The excitement I once derived from solving complex problems and contributing to an innovative environment had given way to a deep-seated sense of discontent.

And anytime I brought up my concerns with my peers, friends, and family they all kept pushing me to stay. I was making great money. I was traveling. I was doing what most 20-somethings would kill for in a role. So I had to figure it out on my own - what did this mean? How do I figure out a path forward and not find myself in this position again.

To navigate this growing sense of misalignment, I decided to sit down and write down what was truly important to me. I meticulously crafted a list of my personal values and career aspirations, hoping to gain clarity on what I wanted from both my professional and personal lives. As I reviewed the results, it became clear that the career path I had been following diverged significantly from the new direction I envisioned for myself. The contrast between my current role and my newly defined values felt stark and disheartening.

The realization left me struggling with difficult questions: Was I giving up? Would people think I had failed? From the outside, I was living the dream professionally. I had achieved a level of success that many would envy, and my career appeared to be thriving. How could I reconcile this outward perception with the internal struggle I was experiencing? How could I admit that I hated my job and needed to leave when everything seemed to be going so well?

The dissonance between my internal dissatisfaction and external success made it even harder to articulate my feelings. The fear of judgment and the concern that others might perceive my decision as a failure weighed heavily on me. I was trapped in a paradox where my career achievements, which once felt so fulfilling, now seemed to be at odds with my evolving sense of self. The challenge was not just in recognizing the misalignment, but in finding the courage to act on it and to redefine my path in a way that honored my newfound values and aspirations.

This realization was not immediate; it crept up gradually as the initial excitement wore off and the day-to-day realities set in. What I initially saw as burnout was, in fact, a signal that my personal values and goals were diverging from the company's trajectory. The intense pressure and lack of separation between work and personal life were not just exhausting; they were indicative of a larger misalignment that could not be resolved with temporary fixes like vacations or role adjustments.

In essence, the vibrant sense of purpose that I had initially experienced was eroded by the persistent demands of this particular startup environment and my growing recognition of this misalignment. The shift from enthusiasm to frustration underscored the importance of aligning personal and professional values, of realizing that just because I had once believed and aligned with . This transition highlighted that what I thought was burnout was actually a reflection of a deeper disconnect between my own aspirations and the company's direction. The challenge lay not in finding a temporary solution but in addressing this fundamental misalignment to achieve a more sustainable and fulfilling balance.

This resentment began to seep into how I viewed my role and myself. The person I had once been—enthusiastic, driven, and passionate—started to fade. I became someone who was frequently exhausted, impatient, and disconnected from my initial sense of purpose. The joy of working in a startup, which had once fueled my career, was overshadowed by a sense of disillusionment. I realized that the burnout I was experiencing was not just about long hours or high stress; it was a profound misalignment between my personal values and the expectations of the job.

The disconnect between my work and personal identity was a particularly painful realization. I found that the more I tried to push through the exhaustion, the more I lost sight of who I was and what I wanted to be. My work, which had once been a source of pride and accomplishment, had become a source of distress. The person I was at work was no longer the person I wanted to be, and this realization was a catalyst for a significant period of self-reflection and reassessment.

I reached a point where I recognized that my unhappiness was not merely a result of overwork but a deeper issue of value misalignment. Despite achieving professional milestones and enjoying financial success, I found myself increasingly dissatisfied as my personal values shifted. This realization was challenging, as it meant acknowledging that the professional goals and achievements I had pursued were not aligned with my evolving personal aspirations.

Ultimately, addressing this misalignment required more than just temporary fixes, such as vacations or salary increases. It involved a thorough examination of my values and goals, both personal and professional. When personal values and professional demands are out of sync, it is essential to explore opportunities that align with current aspirations and provide a better fit for one's evolving goals.

The concept of burnout in the context of startup work often reflects a deeper issue of misalignment between personal and professional values. The startup culture, while fostering innovation and exciting opportunities, can also walk a thin line between being a breeding ground for groundbreaking ideas and becoming toxic through unrealistic expectations and excessive demands. When personal and professional values are aligned, even the most challenging work environments can become manageable. However, when there is a fundamental disconnect, it can lead to persistent dissatisfaction and a need for a more significant change. Recognizing and addressing this misalignment is crucial for finding a fulfilling and balanced work experience that supports both personal and professional goals.

Understanding and navigating the complexities of work environments, particularly in startups, requires a nuanced approach that goes beyond surface-level solutions. By acknowledging and addressing the deeper issues of value misalignment and the potential toxicity of startup culture, individuals can find greater satisfaction and fulfillment in their careers, even in the face of challenging and demanding work environments.

3

Validation: The Elusive Quest

I have always struggled with seeking external validation, a pattern that seems to stem from my years as an athlete, a top student, and maybe, just maybe, a bit from the fact that I'm a middle child. From a young age, my achievements and self-worth were often reflected through the accolades and recognition I received from others. When I worked diligently in softball and made it onto an elite travel team, the acknowledgment of being part of that prestigious group was immensely gratifying especially when I got to walk around a tournament with gear from a team younger girls one day hoped to be asked to try out for. Similarly, my academic efforts were rewarded with top grades, placements on the honor roll, induction into the National Honor Society, and various certificates of achievement. These early experiences set a precedent for my career, where I continued to seek validation through promotions, salary increases, and external praise.

As I advanced in my professional life, particularly as I climbed the corporate ladder, or jungle gym, in my case because nothing in the startup world is a straight climb, the nature of validation shifted. In the earlier stages of my career, the recognition I received from others, such as positive feedback from supervisors and peers, served as a significant source of motivation and affirmation. However, as I moved into higher-level roles, the frequency of this external validation decreased. A shift from seeking acknowledgment of my growth to the expectation that I should independently find motivation and validation marked this transition. The validation I once received was no longer forthcoming because, at a certain level, the focus shifted from personal growth to helping others recognize their own potential.

This shift—from seeking external validation to self-validation—is a critical aspect of personal and professional development, yet it is rarely discussed or adequately prepared for. The transition can be particularly jarring if you have not cultivated the ability to validate yourself. The sudden absence of external praise or recognition can lead to a profound sense of inadequacy or the erroneous belief that you are underperforming. This experience is especially challenging in small businesses and startups, where rapid growth often catapults individuals into leadership roles with minimal guidance or support.

In these environments, the speed of growth can strip you of traditional sounding boards and sources of validation that you once relied on. As you rise through the ranks, you often find that the people you previously turned to for advice and feedback—mentors, peers, or supervisors—are no longer as accessible or present. Instead, you might find yourself in a position where others turn to you for guidance, making the experience of misalignment even more acute, expediting the feeling of burnout. The pressure to provide direction and support to others, while simultaneously grappling with the absence of your own support network, can be overwhelming.

Having frequently been in such roles, I have often faced situations where my peers, or even CEOs, have had less experience in managing complex challenges, such as layoffs, hiring, or setting organizational expectations, compared to my own. This disparity can create a sense of isolation, as you may find that those around you are not equipped to offer the feedback or validation you need. The role of a leader often involves navigating these challenges largely on your own, with fewer opportunities to receive the external validation that once played a significant role in your professional life.

Losing sounding boards and the responsibility of leading others without sufficient support can exacerbate the feeling of misalignment. The absence of regular, constructive feedback and the increased isolation from peers and mentors can make it harder to gauge your performance and maintain a sense of direction. This can be particularly difficult when you are used to relying on external validation to measure your success and progress.

In such circumstances, it becomes crucial to develop the ability to self-validate and to find internal sources of motivation and affirmation. Building a strong sense of self-awareness and confidence in your own capabilities is essential. It is also important to seek out new ways to connect with peers and mentors, even if it means creating new networks or finding alternative sources of feedback. Ultimately, learning to navigate these challenges and finding ways to self-validate will enable you to thrive despite the absence of external validation and support.

This transition from external to internal validation is often challenging, but it becomes even more complex as you grow in your career and assume greater responsibilities. As you climb higher in an organization, particularly in smaller or rapidly growing companies, you often become the proverbial "captain of the ship." The responsibility that comes with this role can be both empowering and daunting. When you are in a leadership position, people depend on you for guidance, direction, and support. This dependency creates a situation where feelings of misalignment, dissatisfaction, or the desire to make a change become incredibly difficult to act upon.

The weight of being a leader means that your decisions and actions have a broader impact on others. You are responsible not only for your own career but also for the well-being and success of your team. This increased responsibility can make it nearly impossible to contemplate leaving a role or making significant changes, even when you feel misaligned or unhappy. The challenge is compounded by the realization that your departure or major adjustments could affect the stability and success of those who rely on you. This sense of obligation can make it hard to prioritize your own needs and redefine your path, even when the traditional markers of success no longer align with your personal goals.

During the COVID-19 pandemic, I worked for a company that seemed doomed from the start. Surviving as a commercial real estate firm during this challenging period felt nearly impossible, especially as more businesses transitioned to remote work and continued that model even as conditions began to improve. As the situation worsened, the company resorted to increasingly unethical practices to remain afloat, prompting me to plan my departure. I attempted to resign on three separate occasions, but each time, I was persuaded to stay—for the sake of my team and our clients. Despite recognizing that leaving was the right choice for me, my sense of duty to support them weighed heavily on my decision to remain.

In navigating this complexity, it's crucial to recognize that success is a personal journey, and its definition evolves over time. While external validation may have once been a significant source of motivation, learning to find fulfillment and affirmation within yourself becomes essential. This means redefining what success looks like for you personally, understanding that it may shift as you progress in your career, and finding ways to balance your own needs with the responsibilities you hold for others. Developing a strong sense of self-awareness and confidence in your own capabilities will help you navigate these challenges and maintain a sense of purpose and direction, even when external validation is scarce and the responsibilities of leadership weigh heavily upon you.

Acknowledging that you are the sole author of your success and defining it according to your personal standards is a profoundly pivotal realization. This recognition shifts the focus from external sources of validation—such as promotions, salary increases, or accolades—to a more internal, self-determined concept of success. It requires you to take ownership of your achievements and to set your own benchmarks for what makes up success in your life and career.

Looking back, I wouldn't change my decision to stay with that company. It didn't experience a miraculous recovery—in fact, it continued to struggle—but staying made sense to me at the time, even if it felt like I was on a sinking ship. While others urged me to abandon ship and seek safer waters, I chose to trust my internal compass over external opinions. I remained not for the sake of the business, but for the people I worked with. That connection and commitment were what truly mattered to me during such turbulent times. A personal value that I had worked to establish as a North Star which stayed aligned with was my definition of success during this time.

Success is not a static or one-dimensional concept; it is dynamic and evolves as you progress through different stages of your career and personal life. What once defined success for you—such as climbing the corporate ladder, receiving formal recognition, or achieving specific financial milestones—may no longer be relevant or fulfilling as your career and life circumstances change. As you advance in your career, your responsibilities, priorities, and aspirations are likely to shift. Consequently, the traditional markers of success that once motivated and guided you might no longer align with your evolving goals and values, something I felt shift during my time at that company in a significant and profound way.

When external validation no longer meets your expectations or aligns with your personal definition of success, it's crucial to take proactive steps to reassess and redefine what success means to you. This process involves reflecting on your current situation, evaluating how it aligns with your core values and long-term aspirations, and setting new, personalized goals. It requires an honest examination of what brings you fulfillment and satisfaction, independent of societal expectations or traditional metrics of success.

Redefining success is not merely about setting new goals; it is about embracing a mindset that recognizes and adapts to the changing nature of your ambitions and achievements. It involves creating a personal definition of success that resonates with your evolving self and ensures that you are pursuing goals that genuinely inspire and motivate you. This might mean finding new ways to measure your accomplishments, such as focusing on the impact you have on others, the work-life balance you achieve, or the personal growth you experience.

Taking ownership of your success and defining it on your own terms empowers you to navigate your career and life with greater clarity and purpose. It allows you to move beyond the constraints of external validation and to cultivate a sense of fulfillment that is grounded in your own values and aspirations. By continually reassessing and adapting your definition of success, you can ensure that it remains relevant and meaningful as you progress through different stages of your journey.

Confronting and accepting the reality that what you initially believed would bring you happiness might not be fulfilling is a deeply significant challenge. It involves a profound level of introspection and honesty with oneself. This process is not just about acknowledging that certain goals or roles may not meet your expectations; it is also about grappling with the discomfort and disappointment that arise when your initial choices do not lead to the satisfaction you expected.

Admitting that you might have made a misstep—whether by taking a job that turns out to be less satisfying than you hoped or by leaving a previous role that you were content with—requires considerable courage. This admission can be particularly challenging because it involves recognizing that the decisions you made were not as ideal as you once thought. It is often accompanied by feelings of regret and self-doubt, making it difficult to confront the reality of having been wrong in your choices.

The willingness to acknowledge and admit that you were wrong about a decision or a path you took is a powerful act of personal growth. It requires setting aside pride and the fear of judgment and accepting that your initial assessment of a situation may have been flawed. This recognition is not a sign of failure, but an important step in the journey of self-discovery and development. It highlights your ability to reflect critically on your experiences and to learn from them.

Taking action in response to this realization—whether by returning to a previous job that you were happier in or by pursuing new opportunities—demonstrates resilience and a commitment to aligning your career and life with what truly fulfills you. It involves making potentially hard choices and navigating the uncertainty of change, but it is also a testament to your willingness to seek out what genuinely brings you satisfaction and aligns with your personal values.

This process of reassessing your decisions and making necessary adjustments is not only about correcting past choices, but also about fostering a growth mindset. It reflects an understanding that personal and professional paths are not always linear and that flexibility and adaptability are key components of long-term success and fulfillment. Embracing this mindset allows you to approach future decisions with greater clarity and confidence, knowing that your ability to navigate and adjust to change is a valuable asset.

Ultimately, the challenge of admitting when you were wrong and taking corrective action underscores a deeper commitment to personal authenticity and satisfaction. It signifies a willingness to engage in continuous self-improvement and to pursue a path that genuinely aligns with your evolving aspirations and values. This journey of self-discovery and growth is integral to finding true fulfillment and achieving a sense of alignment in both your career and personal life.

It is crucial to recognize that external validation, while gratifying, is not the ultimate measure of success. Finding contentment in your achievements and defining success on your own terms is vital. This process may involve making tough decisions, such as leaving a position that no longer meets your expectations or revisiting a former role that you now realize was a better fit. Redefining success and understanding that failure or dissatisfaction is not a reflection of your worth, but a sign that you need to realign your goals is an integral part of personal and professional development. Remember, you are the author of your own story. Do not rely on external validation to guide you; instead, take charge of your narrative and define success on your own terms.

4

The PTO Paradox

In many small businesses and startups, the topic of personal time off (PTO) is a recurring conversation. How do we design a PTO policy that works for everyone? How do we implement it effectively? And, crucially, how do we encourage employees to actually take their PTO? And, the question that's never asked, if PTO is the answer to people feeling burnt out?

I think we all know the answer to this though: nope.

Yet, it remains to be one of the most perplexing aspects of running a business. This challenge is often seen as a peculiar quirk of startup culture, especially when compared to the more straightforward approach found in large, traditional corporate settings. In established companies, employees generally have well-defined PTO policies that accrue over time, making taking time off relatively seamless. Employees in these organizations are accustomed to planning vacations and taking time off without significant hesitation or guilt.

In traditional corporate settings, PTO policies are typically structured and well-defined. Employees earn PTO days based on their length of service, job level, or a combination of factors. This accrual system provides employees with a clear understanding of how much time off they have earned and when they can use it. Companies often have formal processes in place for requesting and approving PTO, which helps to manage workload and ensure that employee absences are accounted for. Their structure enables employees to effectively plan time off and customize it to meet their personal needs, fostering a healthy work-life balance. This support makes it easier to identify any misalignments, as the well-designed system mitigates the symptoms of burnout. When everything is aligned in their favor, employees are more likely to notice when something feels off, essentially making the concern of being burnt out null and void. Everything is designed to ensure they don't feel that way so if something feels off, it's probably more than taking a vacation.

The culture in these organizations also, generally, supports taking time off. Leadership models this behavior by using their own PTO and encouraging employees to do the same. As a result, taking vacations or extended breaks is normalized and expected, contributing to a healthier work-life balance.

In stark contrast, startups frequently offer unlimited PTO, but this policy can come with its own set of challenges. While the idea of unlimited PTO is attractive and theoretically allows for flexibility and balance, it often fails to achieve its intended purpose in practice. The culture in many startups can inadvertently discourage employees from fully using their PTO for several reasons:

- **Culture of Overwork:** Startups often thrive on a culture of overwork and intense dedication. The fast-paced, high-stakes environment creates an implicit expectation for employees to be constantly available and engaged. This culture can make it difficult for employees to take extended breaks without feeling like they are falling behind or not contributing enough.

- **Unclear Boundaries:** Unlike traditional PTO policies, unlimited PTO lacks clear boundaries and metrics. Employees may be unsure about what makes up an appropriate amount of time off or how much PTO is considered acceptable. This ambiguity can lead to uncertainty and hesitation about taking time off, as employees may fear crossing an invisible line.
- **Guilt and Pressure:** Employees in startups often experience guilt about taking time off. They may worry about the impact of their absence on their team, the perception of their commitment, or the potential delay in project progress. A culture that prizes constant hustle and availability can exacerbate this guilt, leading employees to avoid taking time off altogether.

It is not uncommon to see employees taking minimal time off beyond occasional sick days or urgent matters. The concept of taking an extended vacation, such as a ten-day trip to London or a week-long staycation, is often rare. Even when employees take PTO, they frequently remain connected to work through emails, Slack messages, and other communication channels. This tendency to stay connected undermines the very purpose of PTO, which is to provide a complete break from work responsibilities.

When I was early in my career, I found this perplexing. At that stage, I didn't have the financial means to take extended time off anyway, and the idea of staying home with no plans didn't seem worthwhile, so I didn't take a vacation for the first 6 years of my career. Typing that now feels absolutely insane, no days off, not one unless I was sick and even then, I always had my laptop. Holidays just meant working from home. There was no such thing as a break.

One of the most significant issues I've encountered as I've grown in leadership roles is the persistent tug-of-war surrounding PTO. On one hand, there's the challenge of encouraging employees to take time off without feeling guilty, a conversation I've had with more top performers than I can count on my fingers and my toes. I've encountered many situations where employees have expressed significant hesitation about taking PTO, driven by fears of missing out on promotions or being perceived as less dedicated to their roles. This apprehension reflects a broader, deeply ingrained hustle culture that equates constant work and visible effort with true dedication and value within the workplace.

In this environment, taking time off is often seen as a sign of weakness or a lack of commitment, rather than a necessary component of maintaining overall well-being and productivity. Employees who subscribe to this mindset may worry that their absence will negatively impact their career advancement opportunities or how they are perceived by their peers and supervisors. They might fear that stepping away from their duties could cause them to miss out on important projects, visibility opportunities, or critical networking moments that contribute to their career growth.

On the other hand, there's concern about whether employees who take extensive PTO might be perceived as lacking dedication or commitment, another frequent conversation I've had in closed door meetings especially around raise and promotion time. This concern can lead to an unfair and misguided evaluation of an employee's commitment. The assumption that time off equates to a lack of dedication cannot recognize that genuine commitment includes maintaining one's well-being.

This problematic mindset fosters a culture where employees feel compelled to work continuously without adequate breaks, ultimately leading to widespread feelings of thinking they're burnout when they actually truly just need time to decompress. When employees are pressured to remain constantly engaged and available, they often forgo taking necessary rest and recovery periods. This relentless work ethic can cause physical and mental exhaustion, decreased job satisfaction, and diminished productivity. But it doesn't mean that the team is actually burnt out; it doesn't mean they are misaligned at all but simply exhausted.

Ironically, the lack of time off is often communicated as a symptom of burnout though, leading to a misguided belief that a vacation or extended break might resolve the issue. However, this is a superficial solution that only addresses the symptoms, not the underlying causes if someone is truly burnt out. The deeper issues—such as an unsustainable work culture, unrealistic expectations, or a misalignment with the business values and direction—remain unaddressed. As a result, the cycle continues: employees may take a vacation, return to work feeling temporarily rejuvenated, but eventually find themselves back in the same pattern of overwork and what's thought to be burnout.

Time off alone cannot remedy burnout if an employee is truly burnt out and not just exhausted. One way to truly know if an employee is one or other is how often they get to a breaking point of needing a break. If taking time off becomes a frequent need for an employee to show up and be their best yet they keep ending up in the same place over and over again once back to work, it's likely burnout. And time off doesn't work because it does not address the underlying issues causing the employee's dissatisfaction or stress. While taking a break can provide temporary relief and a chance to recharge, it does not tackle the root causes of burnout, which often stem from deeper organizational or personal issues. If an employee's time off is primarily focused on escaping their current situation or merely serves as a temporary respite from ongoing stress, then there are likely more significant issues at play that need to be addressed.

Burnout is a complex condition that arises from prolonged exposure to high levels of stress, excessive workloads, and a lack of support or balance. Simply taking time off does not resolve these foundational problems. Instead, it provides a momentary escape that may offer temporary relief but does not address the persistent pressures or systemic factors contributing to burnout. For time off to be truly effective, it needs to be coupled with a deeper evaluation and remediation of the factors leading to burnout. These issues might include unrealistic expectations, insufficient support, lack of work-life balance, or a toxic work culture. Without addressing these core problems, the cycle of stress and burnout is likely to continue, and the temporary relief provided by time off will only be a short-term fix.

To effectively combat burnout, organizations need to focus on creating a supportive work environment that addresses the root causes of stress. This involves evaluating and adjusting workloads, providing adequate resources and support, fostering a culture that values work-life balance, and addressing any systemic issues that contribute to employee dissatisfaction. Time off should be viewed as an opportunity to recharge and gain perspective, but it must be accompanied by efforts to resolve the underlying issues that contribute to burnout if an organization wishes to retain its talent. What it can't solve is a personal misalignment with the company's values, mission, or business direction - if those are clear and the issues persist, the employee has to decide if they can realign or settle that the misalignment will never change and it's time to leave.

When employees express a desire to take PTO because of burnout, it is crucial to delve deeper into the root causes of their stress rather than simply granting the time off. While PTO can provide necessary respite and recovery, it is often not a comprehensive solution to the underlying issues causing burnout. Addressing the core problems contributing to burnout requires a more nuanced approach, involving conversations about workload, expectations, and work-life balance. By focusing on these foundational issues, we can ensure that PTO becomes an effective part of a broader strategy to sustain and enhance employee well-being.

The first step in addressing burnout is to have an open and honest conversation with the employee. This discussion should explore various aspects of their work experience, including their current workload, the clarity of their role expectations, and their overall work-life balance. For many employees, burnout stems from a combination of factors, such as excessive workloads, unclear expectations, or a lack of support. By understanding these underlying issues, we can develop a plan to address them and create a more supportive work environment.

One critical aspect to explore is the employee's workload. Are they overwhelmed with tasks that exceed their capacity? Are they frequently working beyond regular hours or struggling to manage competing priorities? If so, it may be necessary to reassess and redistribute responsibilities to ensure a more manageable workload. This could involve delegating tasks, adjusting deadlines, or providing additional resources or support to help the employee handle their responsibilities more effectively.

Another important factor is the clarity of role expectations. Employees who are unsure of what is expected of them or who face conflicting demands may experience increased stress and frustration. It is essential to provide clear and consistent expectations regarding job responsibilities, performance standards, and goals. Regular feedback and communication can help employees understand how their work aligns with organizational objectives and provide guidance on areas for improvement. Ensuring that employees clearly understand their role can reduce uncertainty and contribute to a more positive work experience.

Work-life balance is also a crucial element to address when dealing with burnout. Employees who struggle to maintain a healthy balance between their work and personal lives may experience heightened stress and fatigue. Encouraging employees to set boundaries and take time for themselves outside of work can help mitigate burnout. Promoting a culture that values work-life balance and supports employees in achieving it can contribute to a healthier and more sustainable work environment.

PTO should be viewed as a tool for genuine enjoyment and rejuvenation, rather than a temporary escape from unresolved issues. When employees take time off, hoping their problems will be resolved during their absence, it shows a deeper issue within the work culture that needs to be addressed. PTO should provide employees with an opportunity to recharge, return to work refreshed, and regain motivation. However, if the underlying causes of burnout remain unaddressed, the cycle of stress and dissatisfaction is likely to continue, even after the employee returns from their time off.

To ensure that PTO is not merely a band-aid solution, organizations need to implement a broader strategy to support employee well-being. This strategy should include ongoing efforts to create a supportive and healthy work environment. For example, regular check-ins with employees can help identify potential issues early on and provide opportunities for feedback and support. Offering resources, such as counseling services, stress management programs, and professional development opportunities can help employees manage stress and build resilience.

It is also important for organizations to foster a culture that values and prioritizes employee well-being. This includes recognizing and addressing systemic issues that contribute to burnout, such as unrealistic expectations, inadequate support, or a lack of resources. By addressing these systemic issues, organizations can create a work environment that supports employees in achieving a healthy work-life balance and prevents burnout from occurring in the first place.

Leaders and managers play a crucial role in supporting employee well-being and addressing burnout. By modeling healthy work habits, providing support and encouragement, and fostering open communication, leaders can help create a positive work culture that promotes well-being. Training for managers on recognizing signs of burnout and effective strategies for supporting employees can also be beneficial in creating a supportive work environment.

Ultimately, the goal of PTO should be to offer employees a genuine break that allows them to return to work feeling refreshed, motivated, and ready to contribute. If PTO is used solely as a temporary escape from unresolved issues, it will not address the root causes of burnout and may lead to a recurring cycle of stress and dissatisfaction. By taking a proactive approach to addressing the underlying issues contributing to burnout and fostering a supportive work environment, organizations can ensure that PTO becomes an effective tool for maintaining employee well-being and promoting a healthier, more productive workplace.

If taking time off feels like an obligation or if it's accompanied by guilt or anxiety about returning to work, then we have a much deeper issue to address. Creating a work environment where time off is valued and truly used for rest and rejuvenation requires a cultural shift that respects the need for balance and well-being.

5

When Success Feels Wrong

I'm always reminded of a phrase that someone once said to me, and I'm paraphrasing and expanding on the words of this great philosopher (who may or may not be Harry Styles but we don't need to talk about that now): everything people say about you isn't entirely true. Whether they label you as horrific or exalt you as the best thing since sliced bread, their opinions only skim the surface of your reality. Sure, you may recognize that negativity doesn't define your worth, but what about the praise? When people tell you that you should be proud of your life, it becomes harder to ignore. If you don't feel that pride, you're faced with the unsettling notion you might be rejecting something everyone else covets.

Consider this: we often perceive burnout as simply needing a vacation or a break from work. However, that belief only scratches the surface. The reality is that burnout frequently signals something deeper—an underlying misalignment in our lives. It forces us to confront difficult truths. Sometimes those truths are clear as day, a red flag swinging directly in front of you that is so obvious you feel dumb for missing it in the first place.

Other times, the thing that doesn't fit, the thing that is no longer serving you, is harder to admit to because it's the thing that you thought you always wanted. For example, if you find yourself feeling out of place in a city that everyone else dreams of, like New York City, admitting that it's not where you want to be can be incredibly challenging. Everyone around you may express envy for your lifestyle, while you struggle to acknowledge your dissatisfaction.

I know this feeling all too well. When I first moved to New York City, I felt exhilarated. I had always dreamed of living in a city bursting with energy, creativity, and ambition. Friends and family often told me how brave I was to leave the familiarity of my hometown in Oklahoma and plunge into the concrete jungle. They expressed awe and admiration for my decision to pursue my dreams in such a competitive environment. I remember standing in my tiny Midtown apartment, surrounded by boxes, feeling a mix of excitement and trepidation. This was it—the place where dreams came true. I was ready to take on the world. Well, me and my two roommates who somehow managed to make a one bedroom apartment work that first year in the big city.

But as the years wore on, the reality of city life began to settle in. New York is a city of extremes: exhilarating one moment and exhausting the next. The relentless pace, the never-ending hustle, and the high cost of living can wear anyone down. The initial thrill began to fade, replaced by a growing sense of isolation. I worked long hours, often in environments that prioritized productivity over personal well-being. I began to question my choices. Was this really the life I wanted, or was I simply playing the role that others expected of me?

Even as I felt the creeping tendrils of burnout, I grappled

with the perception of my life. People envied my lifestyle and the opportunities that came with living in such an iconic city. They would say, "You're so lucky! Look at everything you've accomplished!" But behind those words, I felt a chasm of disconnect. I was living in a city that many people viewed as the pinnacle of success, and for all purposes, I was succeeding in that city far beyond my wildest dreams, yet I felt increasingly out of alignment with my surroundings. Each time someone praised my life in NYC, I felt like a fraud. How could I tell them that beneath the surface, I was struggling and maybe, just maybe, I wanted to leave?

It's one thing to feel out of sync with yourself; it's another to acknowledge it openly, especially when everyone around you is applauding your choices. The fear of disappointing others weighed heavily on me. Would they understand? Would they judge me? What would they say if I admitted that, despite having achieved what so many only dreamed of, I was unfulfilled? The irony was palpable: I had traded my small-town life for the glittering allure of New York, yet I often felt like I was merely existing rather than truly living.

After nearly ten years in the city, I made the difficult decision to leave. Returning to Oklahoma felt like admitting defeat. People thought I was crazy; they had watched me navigate the treacherous waters of New York City, building a life and a career that many would kill for. "You've made it there! Why would you throw that all away?" they asked, incredulous. Their disbelief echoed in my mind, amplifying the internal conflict I faced. I had built something substantial in New York, yet the weight of that success was suffocating me. I felt like I was wearing a mask, pretending to be someone I was not, and I was finally ready to take it off.

As I packed my belongings and prepared for this monumental change, I couldn't shake the feeling of judgment that surrounded me. Friends were genuinely concerned. They wanted to know why I would leave behind a city that had given me so much opportunity. I could see the confusion on their faces, the concern etched in their expressions. "Are you sure you want to do this?" they asked. "You've worked so hard to build a life there." And as they voiced their concerns, I felt the weight of their expectations bearing down on me. It was a familiar feeling: the pressure to conform to a narrative that didn't align with my truth.

I realized that my decision to leave was not just about geography; it was about reclaiming my narrative. I had spent years chasing a dream that was not entirely my own, and in doing so, I had lost touch with what truly mattered to me. The fear of failure loomed large, but I recognized that true failure would be to continue living a life that didn't resonate with my heart.

Returning to Oklahoma brought its own challenges, but it also offered a sense of relief. I was able to reconnect with the simplicity of life outside the urban grind. I could breathe again. As I settled back into a familiar rhythm, I rediscovered what I valued most: meaningful connections, a slower pace, and the opportunity to explore passions that had been buried beneath the weight of city life.

The skepticism I faced from others didn't disappear overnight, but I started to develop a stronger sense of self. I learned to embrace my choices, regardless of whether they aligned with others' expectations. Each day, I reminded myself that my journey was uniquely mine. It was liberating to let go of the need for external validation and to trust that I was charting my own course.

As I reflected on my time in New York City, I came to understand that burnout is often a signal of something deeper—an invitation to reassess our lives and realign with our true selves. My years in the city had taught me valuable lessons about resilience, courage, and the importance of authenticity. The pressure to succeed in a place like New York can be intoxicating, but it can also blur the lines between our desires and societal expectations.

In acknowledging my dissatisfaction, I learned to listen to my inner voice. The decision to leave was not a retreat, but a courageous step toward self-discovery. Each moment of doubt, each judgment from others, became an opportunity to reaffirm my commitment to my own truth. I realized that fulfillment comes not from adhering to a prescribed path, but from forging my own.

Now, as I navigate this new chapter in Oklahoma, I carry with me the lessons learned in New York City. I've learned that it's okay to let go of what no longer serves us, even if it means defying expectations. Life is too precious to spend chasing someone else's version of success. Each time I face a choice, I remind myself that my journey is not meant to look like anyone else's. It's mine, and that makes it inherently valuable.

As you embark on your own journey of self-discovery, I encourage you to examine the sources of your burnout. Consider what aspects of your life feel misaligned. Are you living in a place that resonates with you? Are you pursuing a career that fulfills your passions? Are you surrounding yourself with people who uplift and inspire you? Don't be afraid to challenge the status quo. Your life is yours to shape, and it's never too late to redefine what success means to you.

The road may be rocky, and others may not understand your

choices, but trust that you have the power to create a life that brings you joy. Embrace the uncertainty and the messiness that comes with it. As you navigate the twists and turns of your journey, remember that every step you take brings you closer to the life that is authentically yours. And as you continue on this path, you may just find that the journey itself is the most rewarding part of all.

It's vital to understand that societal expectations can cloud our judgment about what we truly want. The pressure to conform to a predetermined path—one that looks appealing on the outside but feels hollow on the inside—can leave us feeling trapped. Imagine being in a corporate job that seems perfect from the outside, but inside, you feel like a square peg in a round hole. It's essential to recognize that you have the right to redefine your path, even if it contradicts what others believe you should want.

As I navigated my own journey, I discovered that the hardest part of realizing this misalignment is acknowledging that it may not come from a place of personal failure. Instead, it stems from a disconnect between your inner desires and the external validation you receive. We've been conditioned to think that success looks a certain way—high-paying jobs, prestigious degrees, and societal approval. But what if those things don't resonate with your true self?

I vividly recall the moment I decided not to pursue law school, despite everyone's insistence that I would excel in that field. The shock on their faces was palpable. Here I was, walking away from a well-trodden path to chase an undefined adventure at a startup—a leap into the unknown. When that startup failed after nine months, I grappled with self-doubt. I questioned whether I had made a colossal mistake by abandoning a secure career for something as uncertain as a startup.

However, that failure taught me invaluable lessons. It opened doors I never knew existed and introduced me to opportunities that aligned more closely with my passions. If I had allowed that failure to define my worth, I would have missed out on the chance to explore a world that truly ignited my spirit. Failure isn't the end of the line; it's merely a chapter in your book, one that can lead you to a more fulfilling narrative.

Many people fear failure, viewing it as a definitive endpoint. But in truth, failure is a part of the learning process. It fosters resilience and encourages us to reevaluate our paths. When you experience setbacks, it becomes easier to rise again because you've already learned how to navigate through challenges. Every "no" and every rejection contributes to your growth, making the next leap less daunting.

It's essential to redefine what success means to you personally. The journey to self-discovery often involves stripping away the layers of expectation placed upon us by others. You must confront the voices telling you what you should desire and instead listen to the whisper of your heart. You might find yourself in a job that pays well but brings you no joy. You might live in a city that feels suffocating rather than inspiring. Acknowledge these feelings, for they are your internal compass guiding you toward what truly resonates.

In the pursuit of a life that aligns with your true self, it's crucial to detach from the opinions of others. We live in a world where external validation often shapes our decisions and influences our paths. Society inundates us with messages about what success looks like, what happiness should feel like, and what dreams we ought to pursue. This can create a distorted lens through which we view our own lives, making it easy to lose sight of our genuine desires. Just because someone else's dream life is your current reality doesn't mean it's what you want.

Many people may express envy for your circumstances, celebrating your accomplishments, your career, or your lifestyle. They see you living in a vibrant city, working in a high-profile job, or enjoying the trappings of success that many aspire to achieve. However, beneath the surface of their admiration, it's essential to ask yourself the tough questions: "Am I truly content with where I am?" "Does this life fulfill me?" "Do I wake up excited for the day ahead?" If the answer is no, it's time to take a hard look at your life.

The journey of self-discovery requires introspection and honesty. It invites you to sift through the noise of societal expectations and to examine the motivations behind your choices. Are you pursuing a career because it aligns with your passions, or are you doing it to meet external standards of success? Are you living in a place that nourishes your spirit, or are you simply checking off a box that others expect you to fill? These questions can be uncomfortable, but they are essential for understanding whether you are genuinely living for yourself or merely fulfilling a narrative scripted by others.

Consider how easy it is to get caught up in the comparison game. We scroll through social media, witnessing curated snapshots of other people's lives—careers, vacations, relationships—that seem idyllic and enviable. In those moments, it's easy to forget that those images often represent only a fraction of the reality. Behind the scenes, those same individuals may grapple with their own insecurities, doubts, and dissatisfaction. The illusion of a perfect life can lead to a pervasive sense of inadequacy, making you question your own choices and accomplishments.

To navigate this landscape, it's vital to cultivate a strong sense of self-awareness and self-acceptance. Learning to tune out the external chatter and focus inward is an empowering process. Embrace practices that encourage self-reflection, such as journaling, meditation, or simply spending quiet moments with your thoughts. These practices can help you reconnect with your values, desires, and aspirations, guiding you toward a life that genuinely resonates with your core self.

Taking a hard look at your life may also involve making hard decisions. It may mean walking away from a job that no longer brings you joy or a relationship that feels more like an obligation than a source of happiness. It may mean reevaluating your living situation and considering whether it aligns with your authentic self. Change can be daunting, especially when it requires defying the expectations of others. Yet, remember that your life is yours to live, and only you can determine what brings you fulfillment.

Ultimately, detaching from the opinions of others is a powerful act of self-love. It empowers you to define your own version of success, one that is unique to you. As you embark on this journey of self-discovery, embrace the uncertainty and be willing to step off the beaten path. By doing so, you open yourself up to the possibility of creating a life that truly reflects who you are, free from the confines of others' expectations. Your happiness is worth the effort, and in the end, living authentically is the most rewarding journey of all.

Feeling burnt out often manifests as a heavy weight, making it difficult to even get out of bed or tackle the tasks at hand. When work begins to feel like a chore, it's a sign that something is misaligned. This doesn't mean you should upend your life and make drastic changes immediately. Instead, begin by asking yourself what specific elements in your life are causing this discontent. Is it your job? Your living situation? Your relationships? Identifying these factors is the first step toward realignment.

To move forward, it's essential to silence the noise of external opinions. Only you can determine what is right for your life. You have the power to define your own success. Embrace the discomfort that comes with change and be willing to take risks others may deem foolish. Your journey doesn't have to follow a predictable path; instead, it can be a winding road filled with discoveries and unexpected turns.

Every door that closes behind you can lead to another door opening somewhere else. The key is to be open to exploring those new avenues, even if they seem unconventional. Embrace the uncertainty of the unknown. You may find that the path less traveled is where you discover your truest self.

When faced with the decision to follow your heart or conform to societal expectations, always choose the former. This is your life, and only you can navigate its course. Remember, the hardest path to tread is the one dictated by others' expectations. Instead, forge your own way, and watch how your life transforms when you embrace the authentic path meant for you.

In this process of self-discovery, you'll learn that every setback is merely a stepping stone toward a future that aligns with your desires. Your story may include chapters of failure, but it's ultimately your narrative. Own it, rewrite it, and embrace the journey. As you step into the unknown with courage, you'll find the light within yourself that propels you forward, igniting a passion that makes waking up every day worthwhile.

6

Breaking Free: Overcoming The Stagnation Trap

As I mentioned in previous chapters, for much of my life, I believed external forces dictated my fate. Promotions, salary increases, job offers—they all seemed to hang in a delicate balance that was entirely out of my control. I allowed myself to become a passive player in my own story, attributing my successes and failures to the whims of others. This mindset rooted deeply in my career, particularly during those times when I felt an undeniable urge for change yet felt trapped in my current situation.

The belief that I was stuck was further complicated by a fear of losing what I had built. There was a nagging thought that taking a step down—whether it was a lesser-paying job, a less prestigious title, or a role that felt like a regression—was not an option. I had crafted a life that seemed to define me, and the idea of tearing it down felt insurmountable. This belief that any change would trigger a domino effect on everything else in my life held me hostage. I knew that a drastic salary change would often necessitate a lifestyle overhaul, and that prospect was terrifying.

But the only thing truly holding me back was my mindset. I had convinced myself that the only way forward was to cling to my current circumstances, which inevitably led to burnout and dissatisfaction. The hardest truth to confront was that I had created my own prison, and the key to unlocking it was within me.

I can recall many moments in my career when I felt utterly stuck. It became a pattern: rather than addressing the core issues that made me feel trapped, I would leap from job to job, always in search of something better. I had become notorious for not staying anywhere for more than two years, and that fleeting milestone felt like a small victory in a seemingly endless cycle of discontent.

I would tell myself that I was moving on to something bigger and better. Yet, deep down, I was fleeing from discomfort rather than confronting it. Each new role would initially feel exhilarating, but before long, I would find myself back at square one—feeling restricted and unfulfilled. It was a cycle that became all too familiar, a pattern I repeated with astonishing consistency. In this whirlwind of job-hopping and self-deception, I found a convenient scapegoat in the world around me. Instead of acknowledging my own role in this ongoing dissatisfaction, I projected my frustrations onto my circumstances, my colleagues, and the very organizations that I had chosen to join.

At first glance, this behavior felt like a self-preservation tactic; I could shield my ego from the hard truths lurking beneath the surface. It was easier to blame my bosses for not recognizing my potential, my coworkers for their lack of support, or the company culture for stifling creativity than it was to confront the reality that I was the common thread in this narrative of discontent. I tried to convince myself that the environment I was in was inherently flawed—be it the lack of growth opportunities, the toxicity of the workplace, or even the inefficiencies of the leadership. This blame game became a refuge, allowing me to avoid the difficult introspection that was necessary for genuine growth.

I would scrutinize everything and everyone around me for the slightest imperfection. Was it really the leadership style that hindered my development, or was it my own reluctance to voice my aspirations? Was the workload truly unbearable, or was I simply unprepared to manage my time effectively because I didn't want to do the work in the first place? I crafted elaborate justifications for my unhappiness, convincing myself that if only I could escape my current job, I would find the bliss I so desperately sought. Each resignation was a dramatic exit, a promise to myself that this time would be different, that this next opportunity would finally fulfill me in ways the last one hadn't.

However, this initial thrill of change was always short-lived. The adrenaline of a new job and the excitement of meeting new people would eventually fade, giving way to a disquieting sense of familiarity. Within months, I would find myself feeling just as constrained and unfulfilled as I had before. I had unwittingly constructed a series of gilded cages, believing that a change of scenery would lead to a change in my feelings. But, as it turned out, the change I craved was not external; it was deeply internal.

Each time I transitioned into a new role, I could feel the echoes of my previous frustrations still ringing in my ears. Despite the shiny new title and fresh responsibilities, the underlying issues I had refused to confront persisted, manifesting in the same feelings of confinement and dissatisfaction. The exhilarating high of starting anew was quickly overshadowed by the weight of my unaddressed discomfort. I was, in essence, running from myself—my fears, my insecurities, and my unwillingness to take a hard look in the mirror.

This realization was both liberating and terrifying. I had been so focused on pointing fingers at external circumstances that I had neglected to examine my own actions and mindset. Each blame placed on the world around me was a distraction from the truth that I was the architect of my own discontent. I had allowed myself to remain in this cycle, escaping through the guise of opportunity while avoiding the crucial work of introspection and growth.

In this moment of awakening, I understood that the key to breaking free from this cycle lay not in finding the perfect job or environment, but in confronting the uncomfortable truths about myself. I realized that true fulfillment would not come from external changes, but from a willingness to take ownership of my choices and embrace the discomfort of personal growth. It was time to stop running and start facing the very things I had been avoiding, and that journey would require courage, honesty, and a commitment to transform my mindset from one of blame to one of empowerment.

This realization forced me to acknowledge a hard truth: I was the common denominator in my repeated experiences of feeling stuck. As the singer Taylor Swift wisely put it, "It's me, hi, I'm the problem, it's me." Recognizing that I was creating my own obstacles was the first step toward transformation. It required me to look inward and confront my fears about discomfort and change.

Taking ownership of my narrative meant embracing the

uncomfortable reality that I was the architect of my situation. I had to ask myself: What did I truly want? Was it possible that my perceived limitations were self-imposed? This shift in mindset was pivotal. I learned that instead of feeling defeated by my circumstances, I could empower myself to change them.

The first step in getting unstuck is recognizing that the journey begins within. It's not always about making a grand gesture or taking a drastic leap. Often, the initial action required is much smaller yet equally significant: it's about articulating what you want. Whether it's a different role, a new team, or even a shift in how you perceive your responsibilities, expressing your desires can set the wheels of change in motion.

I will never forget the moment I had to confront my own reluctance to step away from a customer-facing role I had embraced for years. Hospitality had been my calling, yet I yearned for something deeper—something that would allow me to contribute to my internal team rather than constantly interfacing with customers. Until I voiced this desire, I remained locked in positions that didn't fulfill me.

Once I realized I was in control of my narrative, I began to take proactive steps toward change. This involved communicating my needs to my superiors, exploring different opportunities within my company, and seeking roles that aligned with my evolving interests. It was about breaking the cycle of self-imposed limitations and allowing myself to be seen in a new light.

Feeling stuck often breeds resentment and burnout. When you perceive your job as a burden, it can become overwhelmingly exhausting. The sense of obligation to remain in a situation that no longer serves you only deepens the cycle of negativity. You may wake up each day dreading the tasks ahead, feeling like you're dragging yourself through life rather than actively participating in it.

But this sense of burnout is also a choice—a choice to remain in a situation that no longer aligns with your values or aspirations. Recognizing that you have the power to change your circumstances is crucial. One day, you simply have to wake up and say, "I'm going to unstick myself, no matter how uncomfortable it feels."

The journey to unstick yourself won't be easy. It may require difficult conversations, lifestyle adjustments, or even a temporary pay cut. You might have to move to a new city, sell your car, or downgrade your living situation. These sacrifices may seem daunting, but they are often necessary steps toward a happier, more fulfilling life.

One of the most challenging aspects of getting unstuck is confronting the lifestyle you've built. If you've tailored your life to fit your job, it can feel like an insurmountable task to shift gears. The fear of what others might think—whether it's family, friends, or colleagues—can hold you back from pursuing what truly makes you happy.

You may find yourself wrestling with the notion of prestige and materialism. Do you value your identity based on your possessions or your job title? In our consumer-driven society, it's all too easy to equate self-worth with external markers of success, such as salary figures, job titles, and the brands we wear. We often believe that achieving a higher income or a more prestigious title will fulfill us, yet the longer we cling to that external validation, the more resentful we can become about our situation.

I experienced this firsthand during a particularly transformative period in my career. I landed a job that catapulted my salary from $65,000 to over six figures in less than a year. At first, the increase in income felt like a dream come true. I could finally afford the luxury apartment I had always wanted, indulge in finer dining experiences, and travel to places I had only seen in magazines. On the surface, it seemed as though I had reached the pinnacle of success; I was living the life that so many people aspire to. However, as time went on, I began to realize that this newfound financial freedom did little to ease the deep-seated unhappiness that was brewing within me.

Despite the money pouring into my bank account, I was increasingly dissatisfied with my job. The corporate culture was toxic, and the values of the company stood in stark contrast to my own. Each day, I felt more like a cog in a machine than a valuable contributor. My role seemed to revolve around meeting targets and generating profits rather than fostering meaningful connections or driving genuine change. I knew in my heart that I wasn't meant to be there, yet I remained locked in this position, convinced that my paycheck justified my unhappiness.

In my mind, I started to rationalize my discontent. I told myself that perhaps I just needed a vacation. A break from the daily grind seemed like a plausible solution to the internal conflict I was experiencing. After all, wouldn't a week of sun and relaxation help me reset and recharge? I believed that once I returned from my getaway, I would be revitalized, ready to tackle the challenges at work with renewed vigor. But as the days passed, I slowly began to understand that a temporary escape would not resolve the deeper issues at play.

What I was experiencing was not merely fatigue; it was a profound misalignment between my personal values and the company's mission. This dissonance created a growing sense of emptiness that no amount of money could fill. Each day at work became a battle against my own conscience, a constant reminder that I was sacrificing my happiness for a paycheck that felt increasingly hollow. I was caught in a paradox where the more I earned, the less fulfilled I felt.

Eventually, I came to the realization that chasing external validation was leading me down a path of disillusionment. The more I tried to cling to material success, the further away I drifted from my true self. My job title and salary, which I had once viewed as symbols of achievement, became chains that kept me tethered to a life that no longer resonated with who I was or who I aspired to be.

This recognition marked a turning point in my journey. I began to understand that real fulfillment comes from aligning my career with my core values and passions, rather than simply pursuing the next shiny paycheck or prestigious title. It was time to shift my focus away from external validation and toward cultivating a sense of self-worth rooted in authenticity and purpose. I learned that living a life that looks good on the outside is meaningless if it feels empty on the inside. True success, I discovered, is not measured by the figures in our bank accounts or the accolades we collect, but by the happiness and fulfillment we derive from our daily experiences.

This dissonance can lead to a crippling sense of dissatisfaction. It's essential to evaluate what you're willing to sacrifice for your happiness. Are you willing to let go of the perception of success in favor of pursuing what brings you joy? This introspection is critical to your journey of self-discovery.

To truly embrace change, you must accept that discomfort is part of the process. The hard truths you'll encounter—whether in the form of hard conversations, lifestyle changes, or career shifts—can be intimidating. However, the question you must ask yourself is: "Am I willing to endure temporary discomfort for long-term fulfillment?"

This is where the power of choice comes into play. You can choose to remain in a situation that drains you, or you can choose to pursue the path that aligns with your passions. This decision is not merely about changing jobs; it's about redefining your relationship with work and personal fulfillment.

When you start to take control of your narrative, you may notice that opportunities begin to present themselves in ways you never imagined. As you open yourself up to new possibilities, you might find that connections flourish and unexpected avenues become available.

This is not to say that the journey will be devoid of challenges. You may face setbacks, obstacles, and moments of uncertainty. Yet every time you step out of your comfort zone, you build resilience and strength. Each small action you take to unstick yourself is a step toward creating a life that reflects who you are and what you value.

Your energy is contagious. The way you approach your life—whether with positivity, enthusiasm, or resignation—can profoundly impact those around you. As you begin to unstick yourself from the confines of your previous mindset, you may find that your newfound energy inspires others to do the same.

In a work environment, this ripple effect is particularly potent. If you're a manager or a leader, your attitude can shape the morale of your team. When you embrace change and exhibit a positive mindset, it encourages those around you to consider their own paths. Conversely, if you allow negativity to fester, it can create a toxic environment that stifles creativity and enthusiasm.

True leaders have the ability to motivate others through their passion and commitment. Even in challenging situations, a positive mindset can inspire a collective shift towards growth and progress.

As you embark on your journey of self-discovery and empowerment, remember that your role extends beyond your personal transformation. Encouraging others to seek their happiness is just as vital.

When mentoring colleagues or friends, remind them that they are not stuck. Emphasize that happiness cannot be given upon them through external circumstances; it must come from within. Encourage them to evaluate their situations and consider what changes they are willing to make for their well-being.

Ultimately, your purpose on this planet is to be your best self. If you allow yourself to remain in situations that don't align with your values or aspirations, you are doing a disservice not only to yourself but also to those around you. Your growth and empowerment can positively impact the lives of many.

Every day presents a choice: to remain stuck or to take the leap toward change. The discomfort of the unknown can be daunting, but the prospect of a life filled with purpose and joy is worth the risk.

As you move forward on this journey, remember that getting unstuck is not a one-time event, but a continuous process. It requires ongoing introspection, adaptability, and a willingness to confront the hard truths about yourself and your life.

You have the power to redefine your narrative, reshape your experiences, and pursue a life that aligns with your values and aspirations. The journey may be uncomfortable, but it is also a profound opportunity for growth and self-discovery.

So, ask yourself: What am I willing to sacrifice to be truly happy? The answer may be the key to unlocking the life you've always wanted. Embrace the journey, lean into the discomfort, and allow yourself to soar. The world is waiting for you to step into your power and discover the incredible possibilities that lie ahead.

7

Redefining Your Measure Of Success

When I embarked on my career journey, my primary goal was simple: I wanted to enjoy the work I was doing. I envisioned a fulfilling job where passion met purpose. However, as I reflect on my prior experiences, I realize I spent more days feeling miserable than happy. Despite the challenges, including a CEO who was a veritable dragon of a human being, I found solace in the people around me. Those colleagues transformed my daily grind into something bearable. I looked forward to seeing them, even if I dreaded opening my inbox to find more emails or text messages from my demanding boss, who seemed to revel in chaos.

As I navigated my career, I found myself caught in a relentless pursuit of advancement, believing that higher salaries and prestigious titles would bring me happiness. Each leap—from assistant to project manager, then junior manager, and beyond—felt like a step up the corporate ladder. Yet, the startup world often rewards quick promotions and competitive pay while leaving a lingering uncertainty; job security was a constant worry.

Looking back now, I asked myself a profound question: Which job brought me the most happiness? Surprisingly, it was the one that paid me the least. This realization struck me as a revelation. I had always thought that reaching a six-figure salary would be the pinnacle of my success—a transformative moment that would lead to unending joy and freedom. Yet, on the day I hit that six-figure mark, I felt more miserable than ever before. The job, which should have represented a dream come true, became a source of dread. I loathed every aspect of it—opening emails, attending meetings, and dealing with the tedious tasks that came with the position. The only bright spot was the camaraderie I shared with my coworkers, who were equally disenchanted.

Admitting that my happiest days were spent making a mere $40,000 was a challenging but essential step in my self-discovery. This realization struck me as profoundly ironic. How could I, in a society that equates financial success with happiness, feel more fulfilled at a lower salary than I did during my most lucrative years? As I peeled back the layers of my career, it became increasingly clear that my pursuit of a higher income and a prestigious title had overshadowed the core of what truly mattered: passion, fulfillment, and a sense of belonging.

During my time working as a manager at a fitness studio, I found myself immersed in an environment that thrived on energy and positivity. I was surrounded by like-minded individuals who shared a common goal: to empower others and create a sense of community. The work was not just about transactions or meeting quotas; it was about inspiring people to lead healthier lives, and that mission resonated deeply with me. In stark contrast to my previous roles in the corporate world, where I often felt like a cog in a machine, this experience felt personal and impactful.

While I was earning less, the role itself brought me a profound sense of joy. I would wake up each morning excited to engage with staff and clients alike, ensuring that our studio ran smoothly and that our members felt welcomed and motivated. The connections I formed with both my team and our clients were genuine and meaningful. They were not just numbers on a spreadsheet, but real people who shared their struggles, triumphs, and aspirations with me. I was a part of their journey, facilitating an environment where they could thrive, and that brought me an immense sense of purpose.

In the fitness world, the rewards were intangible but invaluable. The exhilaration of seeing our studio's members achieve their fitness goals, the heartfelt gratitude expressed by clients who appreciated our supportive environment, and the camaraderie among colleagues created an atmosphere that was deeply fulfilling. I found myself laughing more, connecting more, and feeling genuinely happy. Those moments overshadowed any concerns about the paycheck I received at the end of the month. The sense of community, the shared victories, and the positive impact on others' lives far outweighed the allure of a higher salary.

However, my journey in fitness was not meant to last. After a few years, I felt the familiar tug of societal expectations creeping back in. Friends, family, and colleagues began to voice what they believed I "deserved." They told me that with my skills and experience, I should be earning more, holding bigger titles, and enjoying the perks that come with a higher position. Their words, though well-intentioned, echoed in my mind like a mantra. I started to question whether I was indeed "wasting" my potential by remaining in a role that didn't come with the financial rewards I had previously chased.

Eventually, I made the decision to leave fitness and return to the hustle and grind of a new and exciting startup. I stepped back into startups, the very realm that had initially burned me out. The allure of financial success and prestigious titles drew me in once more, as did the promise of security that came with them. Yet, I quickly found myself back in environments that left me questioning everything I had learned during my time in fitness. The cycle of stress, dissatisfaction, and burnout began anew.

As I navigated this return to startups, the dissonance between my internal happiness and external achievements became increasingly palpable. I found myself trapped in a whirlwind of meetings, deadlines, and performance metrics, with little time to engage meaningfully with colleagues or clients. A constant sense of pressure to meet expectations and prove my worth through productivity and results replaced the satisfaction I had once experienced in the fitness studio. I realized that despite the shiny job title and the salary increase; I was once again feeling empty.

The disconnect between my external life and internal feelings became impossible to ignore. I was caught in a cycle of burnout, where the pressure to maintain a facade of success weighed heavily on my shoulders. I was in roles that demanded my time, energy, and mental capacity, yet left me feeling unfulfilled. I was too exhausted to enjoy the very things I once loved about my career—whether it was brainstorming innovative ideas, collaborating with talented colleagues, or simply celebrating small victories.

This realization was a pivotal moment for me. I came to understand that I had left a place of genuine fulfillment in pursuit of what I thought I should be doing. The glamorous lifestyle I had created—filled with travel, luxury hotels, and an impressive job title—seemed at odds with my internal experience. I felt like an imposter, surrounded by people who thought I was living the dream when, in reality, I was deeply unhappy. The external markers of success, which I once believed defined my worth, no longer held any significance. I had to confront the uncomfortable truth that my professional happiness didn't correlate with my income. Instead, it stemmed from the meaningful connections I forged and the passion I felt for my work.

Working as a manager in the fitness studio was a breath of fresh air. I was no longer measuring my worth by the size of my paycheck or the prestige of my title. Instead, I found fulfillment in the day-to-day interactions and the meaningful relationships I built. I became adept at managing a team, ensuring that we provided an exceptional experience for our clients, and fostering a culture of support and positivity. Each time I helped a member navigate their challenges or celebrate their milestones, no matter how small, I was reminded of why I loved this work in the first place: it was about lifting others up, fostering a sense of community, and encouraging people to become the best versions of themselves.

As I embraced this new perspective, I began to understand that happiness is not a linear path. The societal narrative often tells us we must strive for more—more money, more recognition, more success. However, my experiences in the fitness industry taught me that fulfillment could come from different avenues, even those that seem less glamorous or financially rewarding. I started to recognize that genuine success lies not in external validations, but in how we feel about ourselves and the impact we have on others.

Reflecting on my time as a manager in the fitness studio, I came to cherish the lessons learned during that period. I learned the importance of surrounding myself with positive influences and cultivating relationships that fueled my passion. I began to seek environments that aligned with my values and allowed me to thrive. This newfound clarity inspired me to take bold steps in my career, embracing opportunities that resonated with my true self, even if they didn't come with the financial rewards I once thought were essential.

This period of my life served as a powerful reminder that success can be redefined. It's not just about titles or paychecks; it's about the joy we find in our work, the connections we build, and the impact we have on those around us. The happiest moments in my career came from pursuing something that lit a fire within me, not from chasing after societal expectations. I learned to listen to my heart and trust my instincts.

In the end, my journey led me to a place of self-acceptance and understanding. I realized that my worth is not determined by the numbers on my paycheck or the titles I hold. Instead, it is rooted in the passion I bring to my work, the relationships I cultivate, and the positive changes I inspire in others. Embracing this new mindset has allowed me to step away from the societal narrative of success and forge my own path, one that is authentic and true to who I am.

Ultimately, my experience as a manager in the fitness studio became a pivotal moment in my self-discovery journey. It taught me that happiness can thrive in unexpected places and that success is not solely defined by financial gain. By shedding the weight of external expectations and embracing my genuine passions, I found a sense of fulfillment that transcended monetary value. The lessons learned during this time continue to shape my career choices and personal values, guiding me toward a future filled with purpose and joy.

This was not my first eye-opening moment about what it truly meant to find alignment in my career; my first encounter with this realization came very early in my professional journey. Back then, I was just starting to navigate the corporate landscape, eager to make my mark and achieve success, which I found in my first startup experience. In the wake of leaving a career in law, I had taken a role at a company filled with some of the smartest and most innovative people I had ever met. I was surrounded by creativity and brilliance, and I genuinely believed I had found my place. However, the company culture took a nosedive when the CEO, in a misguided attempt at humor or publicity, posted a video of a client—naked on the beach—across all our social media channels. It was intended to be "good PR." I was astounded. What was meant to be a lighthearted approach to marketing quickly turned into a public relations nightmare that led to outrage, backlash, and ultimately the demise of our company. It was a stark reminder that no matter how talented the team, leadership decisions could unravel everything in an instant.

Here I was, working with extraordinary individuals, only to watch our efforts crumble under the weight of reckless decisions made by the person who was supposed to care the most about the company. This incident was a sobering lesson, even if the lesson didn't make sense to me until many years later.

For years, I had believed life was a linear ladder, where each rung upward represented success. My upbringing had instilled in me the notion that I should always strive for the next level, never considering that there might be merit in lateral moves or even steps back. One day, a manager of mine shared a different perspective: life is more like a maze or a jungle gym. Sometimes, we must move sideways or even downwards to find our way back up. This metaphor opened my eyes to the reality that my career path didn't have to be strictly upward to be meaningful or fulfilling.

The realization hit me hard: the more I climbed the corporate jungle gym, the less happy I became. It was as if I had been chasing a mirage, convinced that success lay in higher paychecks and fancier titles. Yet, in my pursuit of these external validations, I lost sight of what truly mattered. I had to confront the uncomfortable truth that my professional happiness didn't correlate with my income. Instead, it stemmed from the meaningful connections I forged and the passion I felt for my work.

I started to ask myself, "What do I genuinely want to do?" I recognized that the thrill of my job titles and salaries no longer excited me. Instead, I craved fulfillment and purpose in my work. I had reached a pivotal moment where I needed to step back and reassess my values and aspirations. I left a well-paying job, making the conscious decision to take a significant pay cut to pursue something that felt more aligned with who I was.

Moving to Los Angeles and starting a job in the fitness industry was met with skepticism from friends and family. "What are you doing?" they would ask. "You've worked so hard to get where you are." I felt the weight of their disbelief and even questioned my own sanity at times. But deep down, I knew this shift was necessary for my growth. The step back wasn't a sign of failure; it was a chance to reassess my life and career trajectory.

This transition led me to a new lifestyle that didn't seem glamorous on the surface. I went from working in tech startups to engaging directly with people in retail, experiencing the satisfaction of building something tangible instead of merely designing apps or websites. It felt like a step back on paper, yet in reality, it was a monumental leap forward in terms of personal fulfillment.

Taking that step back allowed me to reevaluate my non-negotiables in life and work. I discovered that my career didn't have to be about climbing the ladder; instead, it could be a journey of self-exploration, experimentation, and growth. The realization that I could forge my own path, even if it confused everyone around me, was liberating.

As I embraced this new direction, I also reshaped my understanding of success. I found that the people I met and the experiences I gained during this time were more valuable than any paycheck or job title. I was no longer defined by how much I earned, but by who I was becoming.

Ultimately, life is not meant to be a rigid ladder; it's a jungle gym filled with twists, turns, and unexpected discoveries. By daring to step off that ladder, I reclaimed my joy and passion for work, even if others thought I was insane. Sometimes, the most courageous thing we can do is take a step back to reassess our values and redefine our path. That leap of faith can lead to a more fulfilling life—one that resonates with who we truly are, not just who we think we should be.

8

The Courage To Quit

In our lives, we often cling to the notion that leaving something behind—be it a job, a relationship, or a dream—equates to quitting. Society feeds us the narrative that if we step away from what we've pursued, we are somehow admitting failure. This perspective is ingrained in us from a young age, creating a powerful stigma around the concept of quitting. We grow up learning that success is synonymous with perseverance, that if we aren't continuously striving, we aren't achieving our potential. But what if quitting isn't the end of the road, but rather a necessary step in our journey toward self-discovery and fulfillment?

Many of us fear the judgment of others when we consider leaving behind what we once thought we wanted. This fear is deeply rooted in our social conditioning, which teaches us that conformity equates to acceptance and success. From a young age, we are bombarded with messages about what makes up a "good" life, often portrayed through the lens of traditional milestones such as home ownership, marriage, and children. These societal markers are woven into the fabric of our cultures, leading many to adopt an unspoken rule that dictates we must check off these boxes to be deemed "successful." As we grow up, we internalize these expectations, often measuring our worth against the achievements of others.

In our hyper-connected world, where social media platforms amplify the curated lives of those around us, the pressure to conform has only intensified. Scroll through your feed, and you'll see seemingly perfect families, dream homes, and picturesque vacations. These images create an illusion of success that can leave us feeling inadequate if our lives don't align with this ideal. We begin to compare our behind-the-scenes struggles with the highlight reels of others, fostering feelings of envy and inadequacy. This culture of comparison can twist into a cage, trapping us in a mindset that insists we must adhere to these conventional standards to gain acceptance.

When we are confronted with the realization that we don't align with these societal expectations, the fear of admitting that we are unhappy can become paralyzing. The internal conflict between what we genuinely desire and what is expected of us creates a heavy burden to bear. The more we dwell on this dissonance, the more anxious we become about the prospect of stepping away from the life we thought we wanted. We may start to question our own validity: "If I'm not married with children, am I failing at life?" "If I don't own a home, does that mean I'm irresponsible?" These questions can spiral into deeper insecurities, clouding our judgment and preventing us from taking the necessary steps to seek fulfillment.

The weight of societal expectations can make us feel trapped in our choices, leading us to maintain the status quo even when it feels detrimental to our well-being. We often find ourselves in situations or careers that drain us, not because they bring us joy, but because we are afraid to deviate from the path that is deemed acceptable by society. The idea of breaking free can be intimidating, as it requires us to confront not only our fears but also the potential judgment of those around us. We may worry about what friends and family will think if we choose to take a different path, one that diverges from the familiar and the conventional. This fear can inhibit our ability to be true to ourselves, forcing us to wear masks that conceal our true feelings and desires.

Many times, our relationships magnify the fear of judgment. The people in our lives who often hold their own expectations and aspirations may inadvertently contribute to our anxiety about making life changes. Friends, family, and colleagues might not understand the internal struggles we face or the reasons we feel compelled to leave behind certain aspects of our lives. This lack of understanding can create a disconnect between our desires and the expectations of those around us, leading to feelings of isolation. The idea of stepping outside the bounds of conventional success can feel like a betrayal to those who have chosen that path, making the act of breaking away even more daunting.

This fear can lead us to self-sabotage. We may make excuses for staying in unfulfilling situations or relationships, convincing ourselves that it's easier to remain in our comfort zones than to risk the unknown. "It's not that bad," we tell ourselves, rationalizing our circumstances as we bury our true feelings. The thought of facing judgment or misunderstanding can be so overwhelming that we choose to endure discomfort rather than seek the happiness we deserve. As time passes, this avoidance can become a habit, causing us to lose touch with our authentic selves. We may live lives dictated by others, measuring our worth against their standards rather than embracing our own unique journeys.

The fear of judgment can also manifest as a fear of failure. When we consider leaving behind what no longer serves us, we may feel a strong sense of loss—not just of the situation itself, but of the identity we've built around it. What if we leave a stable job to pursue our passion and fail? What if we end a long-term relationship and find ourselves alone? These fears can be paralyzing, leading us to stay in situations that stifle our growth and prevent us from living authentically. The prospect of failure can feel insurmountable, keeping us locked in a cycle of inaction.

However, it is crucial to recognize that these fears, while valid, often stem from an external perception of success rather than our own understanding of what it means to live a fulfilled life. By allowing the opinions of others to dictate our choices, we risk sacrificing our happiness for the sake of maintaining an image. In this way, the very fear that holds us back can also become a catalyst for change. Acknowledging that these judgments exist can empower us to confront them head-on.

To begin the process of overcoming this fear, we must first cultivate self-awareness. This involves reflecting on our values, desires, and aspirations. What does success truly mean to us? What brings us joy and fulfillment? By exploring these questions, we can separate our genuine desires from societal expectations. The more we understand ourselves, the easier it becomes to let go of the fear of judgment.

Another important step is to surround ourselves with supportive individuals who encourage our growth rather than stifle it. This may mean reevaluating our relationships and distancing ourselves from those who perpetuate feelings of inadequacy. By fostering a community of like-minded individuals who embrace authenticity, we can create a safe space to explore our true selves without fear of judgment.

Practicing self-compassion can help ease the burden of external expectations. It's essential to remind ourselves that it's okay to make choices that align with our values, even if they differ from the norm. We must learn to be kind to ourselves during this journey, acknowledging that it's natural to experience fear and uncertainty when contemplating significant life changes.

Ultimately, the path to authenticity is about prioritizing our own happiness over societal expectations. It's about embracing our unique journeys and recognizing that the definition of success is not one-size-fits-all. By confronting the fear of judgment and allowing ourselves to let go of what no longer serves us, we can break free from the constraints of conventional success and step into a life that resonates with our true selves.

While the fear of judgment can feel paralyzing, it is essential to remember that our happiness is paramount. The journey toward self-discovery and fulfillment often requires us to challenge societal norms and embrace our individuality. By prioritizing our values and desires, we can navigate our unique paths, free from the shackles of external expectations. The journey may be difficult, but it is ultimately worth it.

The truth is, it takes immense courage to admit that what we once aspired to may no longer serve us. It is in this acknowledgment that we can begin to unravel the layers of expectation and societal pressure that have been placed upon us. It's essential to remember that the only timeline that matters is your own. Each person's path is unique, and the beauty of life lies in its diversity.

Admitting that you need to change course is daunting, but it's a crucial step in finding your true self. Society encourages us to maintain a façade of success and happiness, often at the cost of our mental health and well-being. Many people stay in situations that don't serve them until they reach a breaking point, unwilling to face the reality of their unhappiness. They fear that if they change direction, they'll be viewed as quitters, as people who couldn't handle the pressure.

This mindset can lead to a lifetime of dissatisfaction, and eventually, to burnout. Burnout isn't simply a result of working too hard; it's a manifestation of being out of alignment with our true selves. When we persist in environments that drain us, we become shadows of who we are meant to be, slowly losing the vibrant essence that makes us unique. This disconnection from our authentic selves can create a profound sense of emptiness, where we feel like we are merely going through the motions of life without any genuine engagement or passion.

Burnout often creeps in slowly, starting with a sense of fatigue or unease. We might chalk it up to a particularly busy week at work or a challenging relationship, but as time goes on, these feelings can deepen. The stressors that once seemed manageable begin to pile up, and we start to feel overwhelmed by even the simplest tasks. We might find ourselves dreading our daily responsibilities, waking up each morning with a sense of heaviness that clouds our motivation. This chronic stress is not just about the volume of work we have; it's about the emotional toll that comes from being in an environment that doesn't resonate with who we truly are.

The pressures of modern life can exacerbate this disconnect. We live in a culture that often glorifies busyness, equating productivity with worth. Our constant drive to push ourselves often comes at the expense of our mental and emotional well-being. We might pride ourselves on working long hours, sacrificing our personal lives in the name of achievement. However, this relentless drive can lead us to neglect our needs and desires, further distancing us from our authentic selves. The irony is that while we may appear successful on the outside, we can feel increasingly empty and disconnected on the inside.

The fear of judgment can keep us trapped in these draining environments. We worry that if we express our dissatisfaction, others will view us as weak or ungrateful. This fear can lead us to wear a façade of happiness and contentment, masking our true feelings to fit into societal expectations. We become adept at putting on a brave face, but inside, we are screaming for relief. The pressure to conform can stifle our voices, preventing us from advocating for ourselves and making the necessary changes to restore our sense of self.

As we continue down this path of self-neglect, the toll on our mental health can be profound. Anxiety, depression, and a sense of hopelessness can become our constant companions. We may struggle to find joy in the activities we once loved, feeling detached from the very essence of who we are. The longer we ignore these feelings, the more pronounced the disconnect becomes, leading to a pervasive sense of dissatisfaction. Our lives can feel like a series of obligations rather than a journey of exploration and fulfillment.

Besides the emotional impact, burnout can have physical ramifications as well. Chronic stress can manifest in various ways, including fatigue, headaches, digestive issues, and weakened immune responses. The body's stress response is designed to protect us, but when it becomes a constant state of being, it can lead to a myriad of health problems. The fatigue we experience isn't just mental; it seeps into our physical well-being, making it difficult to muster the energy to engage with life.

To combat burnout, it is essential to recognize the signs early on. Acknowledging our feelings of exhaustion, frustration, or disconnection is the first step in reclaiming our authenticity. It requires a willingness to confront the truth of our situation, even if it is uncomfortable. This may mean reevaluating our choices and taking stock of the environments we inhabit. Are they nurturing and supportive, or do they drain our energy and passion?

Finding alignment with our true selves often requires significant changes. This may involve leaving a job that no longer serves us, stepping away from toxic relationships, or reassessing our life goals. While these changes can be daunting, they are necessary for reclaiming our sense of purpose and fulfillment. It is vital to understand that prioritizing our well-being is not a selfish act; it is an essential component of living an authentic life.

In this journey toward alignment, self-care plays a crucial role. Taking the time to nurture ourselves, whether through physical activity, creative expression, or mindfulness practices, allows us to reconnect with our true selves. It is about creating a space where we can reflect on our desires, dreams, and aspirations without the noise of external expectations clouding our judgment. By engaging in self-care, we begin to replenish our energy and cultivate a deeper understanding of who we are.

Seeking support from others can be invaluable in this process. Whether through friends, family, or professional counseling, having a support system can help us navigate the complexities of our feelings. These connections can provide validation, encouragement, and perspective as we work to realign our lives with our authentic selves. Sharing our experiences with those who understand can help lift the weight of isolation, reminding us that we are not alone in our struggles.

As we begin to take steps toward realignment, we may find that our passions and interests reemerge. What once felt lost can resurface as we create space for exploration and creativity in our lives. This process can be liberating, as it allows us to embrace new experiences and opportunities that resonate with our true selves. It is about rediscovering the joy and excitement that life has to offer when we are in alignment with whom we are.

Ultimately, the journey toward reclaiming our authentic selves requires courage and commitment. It may involve stepping into the unknown and facing the fear of judgment from others, but the rewards are immeasurable. By prioritizing our well-being and choosing to live in alignment with our true selves, we can cultivate a life filled with joy, fulfillment, and purpose. We become empowered to break free from the constraints of societal expectations and embrace the beauty of our unique journeys.

Burnout is not merely a product of hard work; it is a reflection of our disconnection from our true selves. When we ignore our needs and persist in draining environments, we risk losing the essence of who we are meant to be. Recognizing this disconnection is the first step toward reclaiming our authenticity. By prioritizing self-care, seeking support, and making necessary changes, we can navigate the journey of self-discovery and create a life that resonates with our true selves. It is a journey worth taking, as it leads us to a place of genuine happiness and fulfillment.

Instead of seeing quitting as a defeat, we should embrace it as an act of self-preservation and growth. It is not about giving up; it is about choosing to prioritize your happiness and well-being. This shift in perspective allows us to view change as an opportunity for growth rather than a failure.

As we journey through life, it is all too easy to fall into the trap of comparing our paths with those of others. The phrase "keeping up with the Joneses" has never been more relevant than in our hyper-connected world, where social media amplifies the accomplishments of others. When we focus on aligning our lives with someone else's vision of success, we risk losing sight of our own desires and aspirations.

When I moved back to Oklahoma after nearly a decade in New York City, I found myself in a world that felt markedly different from the one I had just left. Surrounded by friends who had taken traditional paths—marriage, children, stable careers—I often felt like an outlier, as if I were somehow falling behind in a race whose rules I didn't quite understand. Their lives seemed neatly organized, each milestone a well-placed stone on a path that led to what society often deems success. In stark contrast, my own journey felt more like an unpredictable river, winding and twisting, without the clarity of a straight road ahead.

This contrast was jarring. As I attended gatherings where conversations flowed effortlessly around parenting advice, school choices, and career advancements, I felt like I was hovering at the periphery, struggling to find my place. My friends spoke with pride about their new homes, family vacations, and the joys of parenthood. Meanwhile, I was still navigating my unique journey, which didn't include these conventional milestones. I was focused on exploring my career, forging new friendships, and discovering what truly brought me joy. But each anecdote they shared served as a reminder that my life was not aligning with the expectations of those around me.

During this period, I grappled with conflicting desires that left me feeling torn. On one hand, I had friends who embraced a more unconventional lifestyle—relationships that defied tradition, careers that allowed for flexibility and exploration, and a willingness to redefine what happiness meant for them. They celebrated their independence, often traveling the world or pursuing creative endeavors that filled them with passion and purpose. Their choices inspired me, yet I also felt the weight of my upbringing, which instilled in me the belief that the traditional route was the only path to happiness and success.

This internal struggle became a source of confusion. I longed for the freedom and adventure that my more unconventional friends embodied, yet I couldn't shake the feeling that I was supposed to follow the well-trodden path laid out by society. It was a dichotomy that left me questioning not just my choices, but my very identity. Was I rebelling against something that might have brought me genuine happiness? Or was I simply trying to carve out a space for myself in a world that felt increasingly foreign?

As I navigated my 20s and 30s, the conflict between these two narratives became increasingly pronounced. I went to college because it was the norm, not necessarily because it aligned with my passions or career goals. I studied subjects that felt practical, choosing majors I believed would lead to stable jobs, all the while feeling a persistent itch for something more. Moving to New York City felt like a bold leap at the time, a departure from the familiar confines of my upbringing, but it was a decision layered with societal expectations rather than my own desires. I was drawn to the city's vibrancy, its pulse, and the promise of opportunity, yet I carried with me the burden of preconceived notions about success.

In this whirlwind of contrasting paths, I often found myself at a crossroads, contemplating the choices I had made and the motivations behind them. I began to ask myself hard questions: Were my choices genuinely mine, or were they merely a response to external pressures? Was I pursuing my passions, or was I simply trying to fit into a mold that didn't resonate with my true self?

It was only in my thirties that I truly began to unpack these conflicting narratives. The realization struck me with a wave of clarity: I had spent my entire life making decisions based on what others expected of me, rather than what I genuinely wanted. I was so consumed by the fear of judgment and the desire for acceptance that I had neglected to explore my true desires and aspirations.

The turning point came when I decided to take a step back and reassess my life. I began to explore what truly brought me joy—activities that made my heart sing and filled my spirit with energy. This process was both liberating and daunting. I realized that I had been living a life that was, in many ways, a performance, carefully curated to meet the expectations of those around me. This epiphany led me to embrace the duality of my experiences.

Yes, I loved the vibrancy of New York City; the art, the culture, the endless opportunities. But I also had moments of frustration and isolation that I had previously brushed aside. The late nights spent working in a high-pressure environment often left me feeling drained, while the relentless pursuit of success felt like a never-ending race with no finish line in sight. I began to understand that every experience is multifaceted; the good and the bad coexist in a delicate balance. Just because something is celebrated by society doesn't mean it is inherently good for you.

The deeper I delved into my self-reflection, the more I recognized the importance of authenticity. I started to embrace the idea that my journey didn't have to look like anyone else's. The unique combination of experiences, relationships, and aspirations that defined my life was worth celebrating, even if it didn't conform to societal standards. I realized that fulfillment doesn't come from following a prescribed path, but from carving out a journey that aligns with who we are at our core.

This shift in perspective was empowering. It gave me the freedom to explore new avenues and take risks that felt aligned with my true self. I started to surround myself with individuals who valued authenticity and encouraged me to embrace my unconventional journey. Their support reinforced the idea that it was okay to step outside the traditional mold and pursue my definition of success.

I began to take small steps toward a life that resonated with me. Whether it was pursuing a new career path that ignited my passion, exploring creative hobbies, or fostering deeper connections with like-minded individuals, I started to redefine what happiness meant for me. This process wasn't linear; it was filled with ups and downs, moments of doubt, and bursts of clarity. Yet, through it all, I learned to trust myself and the choices I was making.

As I navigated this journey of self-discovery, I found solace in the understanding that life is not a competition. Each person's path is unique, shaped by their experiences, values, and dreams. I began to celebrate the diversity of journeys around me, appreciating that my friends' traditional paths were valid and fulfilling for them, even if they didn't resonate with my own desires. I learned that success isn't a one-size-fits-all concept but a deeply personal journey each individual must undertake on their own terms.

Ultimately, moving back to Oklahoma became a pivotal moment in my life. It served as a catalyst for introspection and growth, forcing me to confront the conflicting narratives that had shaped my decisions for so long. In embracing my unique journey, I found the courage to live authentically, free from the weight of societal expectations. This journey of self-discovery has taught me it's never too late to reassess our paths, redefine success, and honor the beautiful complexity of our individual experiences.

Self-reflection is a powerful tool in the process of understanding our desires. Taking the time to assess what truly makes us happy, what feels right, and what aligns with our core values is essential. I began to ask myself critical questions: What do I genuinely want? What are the aspects of my life that no longer serve me? What dreams did I hold onto out of obligation rather than desire?

Through self-reflection, I explored the questions that weighed heavily on my heart. I realized I didn't want the traditional life that everyone around me seemed to value. The conventional markers of success—home ownership, stable careers, and the pursuit of a conventional family life—felt increasingly distant from my vision for happiness. Instead, I found myself yearning for experiences that would enrich my life in ways that transcended material possessions. I craved adventures that would take me to new places, allowing me to immerse myself in different cultures and perspectives. I wanted the freedom to explore my passions without the constraints of rigid expectations, to embrace spontaneity and the thrill of the unknown. This longing for a non-traditional lifestyle illuminated a path that felt true to who I was at my core.

Yet, as I reflected on these desires, I began to understand a fundamental truth: while this is what I want now; it doesn't mean that my desires won't change in the future. Life is inherently fluid, shaped by our experiences, growth, and the passage of time. Just as I had shed the expectations of my past, I recognized my aspirations would likely evolve as I continued on my journey. Embracing this notion of change became liberating. It allowed me to let go of the pressure to have everything figured out and to accept that it was perfectly okay to evolve.

The fear of making a choice that might later feel limiting can be daunting. Society often glorifies the idea of having a clear, unwavering path, yet the reality is that most people's journeys are anything but linear. Acknowledging that my desires might shift over time opened up a realm of possibilities. I could pursue the adventures and experiences that called to me now while remaining open to the idea that my priorities might shift in the years to come. This perspective alleviated the weight of indecision and allowed me to step into my current desires fully.

For instance, the desire for freedom and exploration doesn't exclude the possibility of wanting a family or settling down in the future. I realized that life can be a tapestry of varied experiences, and there's beauty in embracing different chapters. The adventure that defines my life today doesn't negate the potential for future desires to emerge, nor does it invalidate the paths that my friends have chosen. Instead, it creates a rich landscape where I can learn, grow, and redefine what fulfillment means at each stage of my life.

This understanding extended beyond my personal aspirations; it also encouraged me to adopt a more flexible mindset when it came to my relationships. I began to appreciate that the people around me were also on their journeys of discovery, each navigating their own challenges and aspirations. Just because their paths diverged from mine didn't mean that their choices were any less valid or meaningful. This realization fostered a sense of compassion and connection, reminding me that we're all just trying to find our way in a complex world.

As I continued to explore my passions, I found that my journey became richer and more diverse. I pursued opportunities that ignited my creativity, whether through travel, artistic endeavors, or through engaging with new communities. Each experience added layers to my understanding of myself and the world, reinforcing the notion that life is an ever-changing canvas waiting to be painted.

Ultimately, embracing the idea that my desires could change liberated me from the confines of societal expectations. It allowed me to step boldly into the life I wanted, fully aware that the journey would be marked by growth and transformation. I no longer felt the need to compare my path to that of others, recognizing that our journeys are uniquely ours, shaped by our experiences, dreams, and the ever-evolving landscape of our hearts.

As I reflect on this aspect of my journey, I feel a deep sense of gratitude for the lessons learned. I have come to appreciate the beauty of uncertainty and the richness of a life lived authentically. This understanding has become a guiding principle, reminding me that while I may have desires today, tomorrow's possibilities are just as valid. I am free to explore, grow, and change, allowing my life to unfold in ways that are true to who I am—now and in the future.

The fear of what others would think held me back for years. I worried that if I voiced my true desires, I would be met with confusion or disdain. I had friends who were living lives that looked picture-perfect on the surface, and I felt a strong sense of inadequacy in comparison to them.

However, what I learned is that everyone has their struggles hidden beneath the surface. The illusion of perfection can be misleading. For instance, I had a friend who appeared to be living the dream, but behind closed doors, they were facing serious financial challenges and unhappiness in their marriage. They felt trapped in a facade they had created, fearing the judgment that would come with dismantling that image.

This realization shifted my perspective. I understood that vulnerability can be a source of strength. By sharing my own struggles, I could open up conversations that allowed others to be honest about their own challenges. It became clear that the fear of judgment is often unfounded; most people are too consumed with their own lives to scrutinize our choices.

Once we begin to acknowledge what no longer serves us, we can start to forge a new path that feels more authentic. This journey requires courage, as it often involves stepping into the unknown. Embracing change can be uncomfortable, but it is also exhilarating. It's an opportunity to redefine what success looks like for you.

We must accept that the life we design for ourselves may not fit neatly into society's expectations. And that's okay. Each person's journey is unique, and the only way to discover what brings us joy and fulfillment is to be open to exploration.

Letting go of what no longer serves us is a crucial part of personal growth. It may feel like a loss initially, but it can also be liberating. It creates space for new opportunities, relationships, and experiences to enter our lives. When we release the burdens of expectation and comparison, we make room for our true selves to emerge.

Letting go of what no longer serves us is a crucial part of

personal growth, and while it may initially feel like a loss, it can also be one of the most liberating experiences we can undergo. When we hold on to relationships, beliefs, or situations that have outlived their usefulness, we often find ourselves weighed down by emotional baggage and mental clutter. The act of letting go can be intimidating, as it requires us to confront our fears and insecurities. However, this very act creates space for new opportunities, relationships, and experiences to enter our lives, enriching our existence in ways we may not have previously imagined.

The process of releasing what no longer serves us can be likened to cleaning out a closet. As we sift through our belongings, we might encounter items that once held significance but have since become burdensome. Letting go of these items can be challenging, as they often carry memories and associations. Yet, once we remove them, we often feel a sense of relief and freedom. The same principle applies to our emotional and psychological baggage. By shedding what is no longer aligned with our true selves, we create room for growth and transformation.

This act of letting go is not simply about removing the negative; it's about making intentional choices that elevate our lives. When we release the burdens of expectation—those societal and familial pressures that dictate what we should want and how we should live—we allow ourselves to step into a more authentic existence. We begin to understand that our worth is not defined by the milestones we achieve or the roles we fulfill, but by our ability to embrace our individuality and pursue what genuinely resonates with us.

Releasing the habit of comparison can be incredibly transformative. In a world that constantly bombards us with images of success, beauty, and happiness, it's all too easy to fall into the trap of measuring our lives against those of others. This comparison often leads to feelings of inadequacy and self-doubt. However, when we let go of these comparisons, we make room for self-acceptance and appreciation for our unique journeys. We learn to celebrate our progress and recognize that everyone is on their path, with their struggles and triumphs.

As we begin to cultivate this mindset, we discover that letting go opens the door to new experiences. When we release outdated beliefs and limitations, we find the courage to step outside our comfort zones and explore the world with fresh eyes. New opportunities may present themselves—whether in our careers, friendships, or personal pursuits—that we would have previously overlooked. By embracing change and being willing to let go, we create a dynamic environment in which growth can flourish.

Additionally, letting go often paves the way for healthier relationships. As we shed old habits and negative influences, we become more attuned to the connections that nourish and uplift us. We may find that certain relationships, once central to our lives, no longer serve our growth or align with our values. The courage to let go of these connections can be liberating, allowing us to form deeper, more meaningful relationships with those who genuinely support us on our journey. This shift fosters an environment of mutual respect and understanding, where we can thrive without fear of judgment or constraint.

As we navigate the process of letting go, it's important to approach it with kindness and patience. Change doesn't happen overnight, and it's natural to experience moments of doubt or resistance. We may find ourselves clinging to the familiar, even when we know it's time to move on. Acknowledging these feelings and giving ourselves grace during this transitional phase is essential. It allows us to process our emotions and recognize that letting go is a journey, not a destination.

Ultimately, the act of letting go is a powerful affirmation of our commitment to personal growth and authenticity. It signals to ourselves that we value our well-being and are willing to make choices that reflect our genuine desires. By releasing what no longer serves us, we take a bold step toward embracing our fullest potential. The path to personal growth may be challenging, but it is also filled with promise and possibility.

In the end, letting go is not just about loss; it's about creating space for new beginnings. It invites us to envision a future that aligns with our dreams and aspirations, free from the constraints of the past. As we continue on this journey, we will discover that with each release comes a renewed sense of purpose and clarity. We can emerge stronger, more resilient, and more attuned to who we are meant to be. Embracing this process will ultimately lead us to a life that is richer and more fulfilling, marked by genuine connections, exciting adventures, and a profound understanding of ourselves.

One of the most powerful lessons I've learned is the importance of becoming comfortable with discomfort. Growth rarely occurs in the comfort zone. It often demands that we confront the hard truths about our lives and make choices that may initially feel unsettling.

When I decided to leave New York City after a decade, it felt like a monumental decision. Many around me expressed disbelief, questioning why I would leave behind what seemed like a successful chapter. However, for me, it was a realization that the city had become a source of stress rather than inspiration.

The path ahead may be unclear, but that doesn't mean we should avoid taking the first step. Each choice we make is an opportunity to align ourselves with our genuine desires. The key is to trust the process and be open to the lessons that come our way.

As you embark on your own journey of self-discovery, remember to keep your blinders on. It's easy to get distracted by the lives of others, but true fulfillment comes from embracing your own path. Stay focused on what resonates with you, and don't be afraid to take the leap.

In the end, living an authentic life is about making choices that reflect who we truly are, not who we think we should be. Embrace the beauty of your unique journey, and give yourself permission to let go of what no longer serves you. When you do, you'll find that the fear of judgment and the pressure to conform begin to dissipate.

As you navigate this process, remember that you are not alone. Many others are on similar journeys, grappling with their own fears and uncertainties. By sharing your truth, you can inspire others to do the same. Together, we can redefine success and create a world where authenticity is celebrated and self-discovery is embraced.

Trust yourself, trust your journey, and allow yourself the freedom to explore the life that is meant for you.

9

Positive Energy: Authenticity As Power

Energy is an omnipresent force that flows through every interaction, illuminating or dimming the spaces we inhabit. In conversations, meetings, and even casual encounters, energy becomes the invisible thread that connects us all. It's no surprise that I often tell people, "The energy is contagious." Many cannot recognize the profound impact of their own energy, mistakenly believing it pales in comparison to those who naturally draw attention and inspire engagement.

In every room, there exist individuals who seem to command attention effortlessly. They don't merely speak; they resonate. Their presence can shift the mood of the room, drawing others into their orbit. Yet, what if I told you that this ability isn't exclusive to a select few? Every person possesses this potential, the innate ability to mold the atmosphere around them. Whether in a boardroom, a family gathering, or among friends, we all have the power to be a contagious force within our circles.

However, this power comes with a caveat. It is essential to acknowledge that the energy we emit, whether positive or negative, influences not only our experiences but also those of everyone around us. This realization can be daunting. Many struggle to express feelings of burnout or dissatisfaction because admitting unhappiness can feel like a betrayal of the good fortune they've been granted. Instead, they lean towards terms like "burnout," believing it to be a temporary fix for a deeper, more complex issue.

Burnout, a term that has permeated our collective consciousness, often serves as a convenient label for a much larger emotional struggle. When we use this word, we imply that our current state is just a phase, something that can be remedied with a break or a vacation. However, this perspective overlooks a fundamental truth: if you consistently feel a dark cloud hovering above you, the root cause of that cloud extends far beyond mere fatigue. No amount of time off can lift that cloud until you confront its origins.

If the only moments you feel light and free occur when you're physically absent from a place, whether that be work or home, it's imperative to understand that this cloud—this heavy energy—is being felt by those around you. Friends, colleagues, and family are not merely observers of your mood; they are participants in it. When you walk into a room carrying that cloud, others instinctively feel its weight, as if they, too, are standing in a rainstorm.

People often react to this energy in attempts to help, offering help or suggesting breaks, which can lead to feelings of inadequacy. When others offer to take tasks off your plate or urge you to take time away, it may inadvertently trigger a sense of helplessness or resentment. It becomes a cycle: you feel the weight of the cloud; they feel your energy, and their attempts to help can make you feel even more isolated. This disconnect can fester into bitterness, eroding your relationships and clouding your spirit even further.

I once found myself ensnared in this cycle. In one of my jobs, I was acutely aware of the dark energy I was radiating. My role demanded a level of enthusiasm and positivity that I no longer possessed. I became a master of disguise, showing up to work with a smile plastered on my face while feeling the internal struggle consuming me. Every day, I would wear my mask, pretending to be happy, all the while feeling like I was carrying the weight of a thousand stones.

As the days turned into weeks and weeks into months, the act of pretending took its toll. The façade began to crack, seeping negativity into my interactions with colleagues and loved ones. I realized that my bitterness was starting to manifest in my closest relationships. People who cared about me would ask how I was doing, and I would deflect, assuring them that everything was fine when, in truth, I felt anything but fine.

This internal conflict festered, feeding my resentment and deepening the cloud above me. The longer I ignored my true feelings, the more pronounced the energy shift became. Those around me could sense the heaviness I carried; it was as if I had become a storm cloud hovering over their heads.

I was reminded of a crucial lesson: your energy is contagious. It can light up a room or cast a shadow over it. This realization came with both clarity and pressure. If my mood could influence the atmosphere around me, how was I allowing myself to remain in a state that was counterproductive to not only my well-being but also that of others?

There's an unspoken expectation that those with influence must always be positive, proactive, and uplifting. It felt overwhelming, this burden of expectation. Yet, I began to recognize that my ability to impact others positively rested not solely on my ability to maintain a facade of happiness. It resided in my honesty and authenticity.

The struggle lies in the fear of admitting unhappiness, as though doing so is an act of ingratitude. We live in a culture that celebrates achievement and resilience. Admitting discomfort or discontent can feel like a deviation from the narrative of success. I often grappled with the idea that to express dissatisfaction was to undermine the hard work that had brought me to that point in my career.

However, I realized that shining doesn't require perfection. Each of us shines in our unique way—whether we are extroverted firecrackers or quiet, reflective souls. Recognizing how we operate and acknowledging when we can no longer shine in our current environment is vital for our emotional health.

In my case, I clung to my job title and salary, viewing them as markers of success. But deep down, I knew that they didn't align with my authentic self. The act of pretending became exhausting, not just for me, but for those around me. Relationships started to fray as I unconsciously projected my unhappiness onto others, and they began to distance themselves from the negativity I exuded.

As I navigated my feelings, I discovered that change often begins with self-acceptance. Accepting that my current situation wasn't serving me was the first step toward reclaiming my energy. I learned to articulate my feelings rather than masking them. Instead of labeling my experience as mere "burnout," I began to examine the deeper roots of my unhappiness.

This realization marked a significant turning point. I recognized that my energy was a reflection of my environment. Just as light can illuminate dark spaces, acknowledging my truth allowed me to identify the shadows within me. This newfound awareness compelled me to make necessary changes—changes that ultimately illuminated my path forward.

The question became: How do we honor our own energy while also considering the impact we have on those around us? It begins with an understanding that it is okay to be selfish when it comes to your well-being. Declaring, "I don't want this job," or "I don't want these responsibilities," doesn't equate to a lack of ambition. Instead, it's an act of self-preservation, a declaration of one's right to seek fulfillment and joy.

This journey caused a reevaluation of what success meant to me. Society often dictates that success is synonymous with titles, salary bands, or climbing the corporate ladder. However, I began to question this narrative. Was I pursuing a title because I genuinely wanted it, or simply because it was the next step? The realization that not everyone is meant to lead or ascend the ranks was liberating.

In a world that pressures us to constantly strive for more, it can feel revolutionary to assert, "I'm happy where I am." This perspective allows us to align our careers with our passions and values. It's important to embrace that we don't have to chase every opportunity that presents itself.

For example, during my conversations with colleagues who expressed dissatisfaction, I would ask, "Do you truly want that promotion?" Often, the response would be a hesitant, "Well, no, but it's the next step." This response highlighted a crucial insight: we often feel compelled to pursue paths laid out for us by others. But what if we dared to carve our own paths, guided by what truly resonates with our inner selves?

Learning to say no is an essential skill in preserving our energy. It's about recognizing our limits and honoring them. When presented with opportunities that don't align with our goals or values, it's okay to decline. The fear of missing out can be paralyzing, yet choosing to prioritize our well-being over societal expectations is a radical act of self-care.

It's not uncommon for people to associate their self-worth with the titles they hold or the promotions they receive. However, I have come to believe that true self-worth stems from understanding where we shine. We all possess unique strengths and talents that contribute to our environments. When we acknowledge and embrace these attributes, we create space for genuine connection and collaboration.

Rejecting opportunities that don't resonate with our true selves does not mean we lack ambition. Rather, it signifies a commitment to authenticity. As we honor our energy and choose paths that reflect our passions, we cultivate environments where we—and others—can thrive.

The energy we project ripples outward, influencing the dynamics of our interactions. When we embrace our authentic selves, we create a space for others to do the same. It's a collective journey toward positivity and empowerment.

By focusing on what truly matters to us, we can inspire others to break free from societal expectations. When we prioritize our well-being and align with our passions, we give others permission to explore their own paths without fear of judgment.

In the workplace, this translates to fostering a culture of openness and authenticity. When leaders model vulnerability, it encourages team members to express their true selves. Rather than suppressing feelings of burnout or dissatisfaction, individuals feel empowered to share their experiences, leading to collective growth and understanding.

Ultimately, our energy is a reflection of our inner selves. When we embrace authenticity, we cultivate an environment where everyone can shine. Recognizing the power of our energy allows us to navigate our lives with intention and purpose.

To truly harness your power and potential, it's essential to reflect on the energy you're projecting. Are you stepping into the world as your authentic self, or are you holding back, perhaps masking parts of yourself to fit into certain expectations or roles? So often, misalignments between who we are and how we show up to the world lead to a sense of disconnect. When we're out of sync with our authentic selves, it can feel like we're carrying extra weight, and our energy doesn't flow as freely or fully. Misalignments create blocks that hold us back, keeping us from truly shining.

Consider how much of your energy might be spent maintaining an image or suppressing parts of yourself to meet certain expectations—whether they're self-imposed, come from others, or are rooted in societal standards. When we're not fully embracing who we are, we're masking the very essence that makes us unique. This not only drains us but also restricts the powerful impact we could have on others. Aligning with your true self is about releasing those limitations and letting your genuine energy shine, free from filters or constraints.

This process of alignment, however, often requires inner work. It involves acknowledging areas where you might feel resistance or where you sense a gap between your actions and your true values. Perhaps you're in a job that doesn't resonate with your core passions, or maybe you're in relationships that don't truly support your growth. These are signals pointing to areas of misalignment, and identifying them is the first step to realigning with your authentic energy.

As you begin to address these misalignments, you may notice a remarkable shift in your energy. Rather than being drained by the effort of maintaining an image or pushing yourself to fit molds that don't serve you, you'll find yourself feeling lighter and more empowered. Embracing who you are fully enables your energy to flow naturally, bringing a sense of ease and confidence that's noticeable to everyone around you. This shift not only elevates your experience but also serves as a source of inspiration to others, encouraging them to step into their own light.

Our energy, after all, is contagious. When we embrace our authenticity, we radiate a positive energy that can uplift those around us. By letting your true self shine, you're making space for others to do the same, creating an environment where authenticity and empowerment are welcomed and celebrated. Imagine the collective impact when each of us brings our genuine selves into the world—this ripple effect has the power to transform our relationships, our communities, and even our workplaces.

Embracing alignment is, therefore, not just a personal journey; it's a collective gift. By allowing your true essence to emerge, you're not only empowering yourself but also making a profound contribution to the energy around you. So, take that step to identify where you might be out of sync, realign with your values, and embrace your unique light. The world needs the genuine, unapologetic you—let that contagious, positive energy flow and watch as it sparks a wave of authenticity and inspiration in others. Let your essence shine unapologetically, and allow it to energize and uplift the world around you.

It may be scary. It may be hard. But you can do hard things and the reward on the other side is worth it.

About the Author

Brandi is an inspiring storyteller and passionate advocate for living life to the fullest. Born and raised in Oklahoma City, she has cultivated a diverse perspective through her ties to vibrant cities like New York City, Los Angeles, and Austin. With over 14 years of experience in the startup world, Brandi thrives on innovation and creativity, always seeking new ways to empower others. Her work is driven by a deep commitment to help individuals break free from the mundane and embrace their true potential. Brandi believes that life is meant to be lived, not just endured.

You can connect with me on:
- https://www.brandijacksoncoaching.com
- https://www.instagram.com/brandi.d.jackson/?hl=en

Made in the USA
Columbia, SC
28 November 2024